Instant Pot® EVOLUTION

100 illustrated recipes for your Instant Pot.
From pressure cooking to sous vide.

Recipes for all models of Instant Pot
Plus sous vide recipes

Graham Sharman
&
James Sharman

Copyright © 2021 Reliable Marketing Limited
All Rights Reserved

No parts of this book may be used or reused in any manner whatsoever without permission except in the case of brief quotations embodied in critical articles or reviews. Thank you for buying an authorized edition of this book and for complying with copyright laws by not scanning, reproducing, or distributing without permission.

INSTANT POT® and associated logos are owned by Instant Brands Inc. and are used under license.

Dedication

In memory of mother/grandmother Phyllis and sisters/aunties Jennifer and Barbara.

Many happy meals shared.

This book is for you.

About the Authors

Graham Sharman

Lots of people use an Instant Pot or pressure cooking to regularly cook the same things over and over. Dad's different. He hardly ever cooks the same thing twice. He's without a doubt one of the most self-critical cooks I've ever come across, (both in and out of professional restaurants). He's been a huge advocate for pressure cooking for as long as I can remember, & over the years has mastered a truly miraculous range of creations via his Instant Pot.

James

James Sharman

I would like to think that I could take some credit for my sons' achievements, but I can't remember preparing him to work with one of the UK's best chefs, cooking in the renowned (best restaurant in the world) Noma, or setting up pop up restaurants across the world including Mount Everest. In all honesty, I don't think that I can. James' experience and advice have been invaluable in creating this book. I'm a lucky and very proud dad.

Graham

Table of Contents

Introduction xi

Breakfast 1
    Easy Yogurt 2
    Overnight Instant Pot Porridge / Oatmeal 3
    Homemade Granola 4
    Sous Vide Poached Eggs 5
    Sous Vide Eggs Benedict 6
    Perfect Boiled Eggs 7

Soup 9
    Scotch Broth 10
    Creamy Courgette/Zucchini & Cheese soup 11
    Minestrone 12
    Moroccan Harira Lamb 13
    Irish Leek & Potato Soup 14
    Moroccan Mushroom & Lentil Soup 15
    Mulligatawny 16

Rice 17
    Plain Rice 18
    Pilau 19
    Coconut Rice 20
    Spiced Mexican Rice 21
    Chicken & Chorizo Risotto 22
    Vegetable Biryani 23
    Egg Fried Rice 25

Pork 27
    Slow Cooked Pork & Pineapple Curry 28
    Sausages in Balsamic Onion Gravy 29

Sweet & Sour Pork with Peppers	30
Braised Pork & Apple	31
Ham, Beans & Orange	32
Pork with Tomato & Fennel	33
Pork & Celeriac	34
Pineapple Infused Sous Vide Gammon Steaks	35
Shredded Pork & Cider Rolls	36
Lamb	**37**
Braised Lamb Shoulder	38
Spiced Lamb with Tomato & Chickpeas	39
Moussaka	40
Rotisserie Döner (Shawarma) Kebab	41
Liver & Onions	42
Summer Lamb with Mint & Tomato	43
Lamb Rogan Josh	44
Keema Aloo	45
Beef	**47**
Texas Red	48
Beef & Beans	49
Beef Stroganoff	50
Seared Steak Stew	51
Goulash	52
Beef Bourguignon	53
Cornish Galette	55
Sous Vide Steak & Vegetables	56
Roasted Beef Spaghetti Bolognese	57
Chicken	**59**
Moroccan Lemon Chicken	60
Chicken Tikka Masala	61
Chicken & Spring Vegetable Stew	62
Chicken Kebab (Shawarma)	63
Shredded Chicken Burger	64
Coq au Vin	65
Sous Vide Ham & Cheese Stuffed Chicken Breasts	67
Sous Vide Piri Piri Chicken	68
Fish	**69**
Smokey fish Stew	70

  Tuna & Tomato Penne 71
  Sous Vide Tuna Confit 72

Salads 73
  Thai Chicken & Mango Salad 74
  Potato & Egg Salad 75
  Coronation Chicken 76

Vegetarian 77
  Zucchini/Courgette & Cauliflower Curry 78
  Scary Squash Risotto 79
  Black Bean Chilli 80
  Ratatouille 81
  Thai Green Tofu Curry 82
  Spiced Sweet Potato Burger 83
  Cheese & Leek Galette 84
  Broccoli Cheese Pasta 85
  Simple Pesto Pasta 86

Sides 87
  Mash in a Flash 88
  Crushed Peas with Mint & Creme Fraiche 89
  Crunchy Cauliflower Cheese 90
  Bombay Potatoes 91
  Homemade Baked Beans 92
  Instant Pot Bread 93
  Sous Vide Chilli Butter Corn 94
  Jenny's Baked Mac & Cheese 95

Condiments etc 97
  Quark 98
  Dark Cherry Almond Jam 99
  Chicken Stock 100
  Bread Sauce 101
  Mango Chutney 102
  Piccalilli 103
  Sous Vide Thyme Infused Oil 104
  Sous Vide Pickles 105

Sweets & Desserts 107
  Baked Granola Apples 108

Traditional Rice Pudding 109
Aromatic Rice Pudding 110
Ice Cream Bread 111
Poached Pears in Cranberry Juice 112
Bread & Butter Pudding 113
Toasted Sweet Coconut Popcorn 114
Marmalade Roly-Poly 115
Autumn Cake 116
Sous Vide Custard. 117
Sous Vide Crème Brûlée 118
Sous Vide Ice Cream 119
Chocolate Mousse 120
Sous Vide Fig Swirls 121
Sous Vide Tempered Chocolate. 123

Acknowledgments 124

Introduction

Multi-Cookers

Thanks to the extreme popularity of the Instant Pot over the past few years, many people are falling in love with pressure cooking, and for good reason.

Electric multi-cookers like the Instant Pot are incredibly fast, they're easy to use, and the food tastes great.

Because the pot is tightly sealed, all the volatile flavour molecules stay in the pot instead of evaporating away, and juices concentrate into rich savoury sauces. Multi-cookers include a sauté function, allowing you to cook a diverse range of dishes, all in the same pot. There's less mess, and you don't even have to turn on the stove.

A multi-cooker is both a frugal choice and a versatile machine, capable of replacing a handful of appliances in your kitchen. In this book, we will work through how to make the most of your Instant Pot as a steamer, rice cooker, yogurt maker, sous vide machine, slow cooker, and much more...

The Instant Pot

The original and by far the best multi-cooker, in my opinion, is the Instant Pot. Great design and build quality, accompanied by a myriad of accessories available are why it's the best-selling multi-cooker on the market, and why I continue to use mine every day after all these years.

If you are new to pressure cooking, I would recommend that you read your instruction manual and fully familiarise yourself with your lovely new device.

Models used in creating recipes for this book are the Duo, and Duo Evo Plus, both 6 quart / 5.7 litres. Cooking times may vary if using 3 quart / 3 litres or 8 quart/8 litres.

Weights & Measures

U.S. cups are used predominantly throughout this book, as they are the measuring standard in the US. Also, I prefer scooping to weighing whenever possible. A set of measuring cups is relatively inexpensive and should last for many years. For weights, imperial and metric conversions have been provided for your convenience.

About This Book

My first experience with pressure cooking was as a young boy. Watching my mother cooking with what looked like a large saucepan with a strange-looking lid. The fright of seeing the valve hitting the ceiling one day put me off having anything to do with pressure cookers for many years after that. Thankfully, times have changed for the better, losing the sight in one eye is no longer a concern. The Instant Pot has so many safety features that you no longer have to worry. It's very easy to use, and each model just keeps getting better.

I started using a stovetop pressure cooker about ten years ago. Its main purpose was to speed up the softening of onions to make restaurant-style Indian curries. A few years later, I bought an Instant Pot, loved it, and have been using it almost daily ever since.

Does that qualify me to write a cookbook though? I didn't think so until I spoke to my son. He insisted that the knowledge I had gained over all these years of pressure cooking, would prove far more valuable to someone who had just bought their first Instant Pot than a general cookbook from a celebrity chef ever could.

He suggested we join forces, my love for the Instant Pot, and his knowledge of cooking.

And so......here is that book!

Breakfast

Easy Yogurt

Stir a few simple ingredients together in the Instant Pot, and a few hours later…

Beautifully smooth thick & creamy yogurt.

No boiling, straining, or thermometers.

SERVES 8

INGREDIENTS

- 3 cups/750 ml whole ultra-pasteurized ultra-filtered milk or ultra-high temp milk
- 1 cup/120g skimmed milk powder (optional)
- ¼ cup/60 ml condensed milk (optional)
- 2 tbsp unopened plain yogurt containing live cultures

PREPARATION STEPS

1. <u>IMPORTANT:</u> Do not use standard milk for this recipe.
2. Pour 1 of the cups/250 ml of milk into the Instant Pot, reserve the other 2 cups.
3. Anything you add at this stage must not contain live bacteria apart from the yogurt containing live cultures as they usually don't interact too well.
4. Stir in 1 cup/120g of skimmed milk powder, ¼ cup/60 ml of condensed milk and 2 tbsp unopened plain yogurt containing live cultures.
5. Whisk until smooth then add the 2 cups/500 ml of reserved milk, stir in.
6. Cover with the lid, don't set to seal, remove rubber seal if tainted to avoid onion flavored yogurt.
7. On your Instant Pot select yogurt.
8. Make sure your Instant Pot is set to normal 8 hours, if it isn't, press adjust until display shows 8.00. Display will go to 0.00 and count up.
9. On Duo Evo Plus select yogurt/custom/8.00/temp 110°/f/43°/c/start. Display will count down once up to temp.
10. After 8 hours, once the Instant Pot has beeped, remove lid, take out inner pot and line the lid with paper towel to stop condensation drips. Replace lid. You can also use a plate instead of the lid.
11. Place in refrigerator for at least 4 to 6 hours
12. When stirred the yogurt will thin down slightly this is normal.
13. Doubling or tripling recipe will not affect times or temperatures.
14. Store yoghurt in the fridge for up to two weeks.
15. Add your favourite fruit or toppings.

Tip: If you are making plain, unflavoured yogurt, you may want to freeze some in ice cube trays to use as starters for your next batch of yogurt.

INGREDIENTS

POT IN POT METHOD

- 1 cup/250 ml of cold water in pot for pressure
- 1 ½ cups/150g jumbo rolled oats
- 3 cups of water or a 50/50 water and nut milk (but not dairy if you plan to leave it in the pot overnight)
- Pinch of salt
- 3 tbsp of your preferred sweetener (sugar, honey, syrup etc.) also a handful of dried fruit is nice and ½ tsp cinnamon
- (anything that won't spoil overnight)

PREPARATION STEPS

1. Place trivet into the Instant Pot, pour in 1 cup/250 ml of cold water into the inner pot.

2. In the oven safe ceramic bowl, mix 1 ½ cups/150g of jumbo rolled oats, 3 cups of water or a 50/50 water and nut milk mix, a pinch of salt and 3 tbsp of your preferred sweetener.

3. Place lid on Instant Pot, set valve to seal, select manual high pressure (pressure cook custom high on Evo Plus) for 15 minutes.

4. If setting the timer, follow the instructions above, then press timer, toggle timer button for hours or minutes, increase or decrease hours and minutes by pressing + or - (for Evo plus press delay start, turn dial to set hours and minutes, press start to begin count down).

5. Quick or natural release is fine, the porridge will be okay left on keep warm for at least half an hour.

Tip: You can cook directly in the inner pot using the same recipe, just change the cooking time to 2 minutes with a natural release until the pin drops. It does tend to come out a bit thicker at the bottom of the pot though and can stick a little.

Overnight Instant Pot Porridge / Oatmeal

Wake up to fresh porridge in the morning.

Let the Instant Pot do the work for you by using the timer function.

Just open the lid and serve.

SERVES 4

Homemade Granola

So much healthier than the shop bought version.

Customise to your own taste.

SERVES 8

INGREDIENTS

- 2 tsp olive oil
- ¼ cup/60g golden syrup
- 1 tbsp honey
- ½ tsp vanilla extract
- 1½ cups/150g jumbo rolled oats
- 3 tbsp sunflower seeds
- 2 tbsp sesame seeds
- 3 tbsp pumpkin seeds
- ¾ cup/50g sliced almonds
- ½ cup/80g dried berries
- ⅓ cup/50g sultanas
- ⅓ cup/30g desiccated coconut

PREPARATION STEPS

1. In the instant pot mix 2 tsp olive oil, ¼ cup/60 golden syrup, 1 tbsp honey and ½ tsp vanilla extract.

2. Add 1½ cups/150g jumbo rolled oats, 3 tbsp sunflower seeds, 2 tbsp sesame seeds, 3 tbsp pumpkin seeds, ¾ cup/50g sliced almonds, ½ cup/80g dried berries, and 1/3 cup/30g desiccated coconut. Hold the sultanas back until later.

3. Stir to combine.

4. Place lid on Instant Pot. Make sure valve is NOT set to seal.

5. Press the slow cook button on the Instant Pot, press adjust to less, and + or – to 1.5 hours.

6. On the Evo Plus press slow cook/custom/1.5 hours/low/start.

7. After 30 minutes, remove the lid and stir the granola then re-cover.

8. After another 30 minutes stir again, this time adding 1/3 cup sultanas. Re-cover, and continue cooking for the final 30 minutes. Press cancel.

9. Remove the lid, stir the granola, and leave to cool.

10. Can be stored for up to 1 month in an airtight container. Don't cover until the granola has cooled completely.

Sous Vide Poached Eggs

One of the simplest things, but so easy to get wrong. Sous vide gives you perfect results every time.

SERVES 1-4

INGREDIENTS

- 1 to 4 large eggs (from the refrigerator)
- Bowl of ice water
- Salt & pepper to season

PREPARATION STEPS

1. Fill inner pot to just below maximum with hot water.
2. Select sous vide mode custom 75 °/c/167 °/f and set time for 12 minutes and close lid with valve open.
3. Once up to temperature gently lower egg(s) (unbroken, shell intact) into the water with a large, slotted spoon and close lid, with valve open.
4. Once Instant Pot beeps, remove the eggs and place them in the ice water or one minute.
5. Gently break eggs and turn out.
6. Season to taste.

Sous Vide Eggs Benedict

A classic dish with poached eggs and (no longer notoriously tricky to make) hollandaise, made simple.

SERVES 4

INGREDIENTS

Hollandaise Sauce

- 3 large egg yolks
- 6 tbsp salted softened butter
- 1 tbsp lemon juice
- 2 tbsp water
- Pinch of cayenne pepper or mustard powder

Poached Eggs

- 4 large eggs (from the refrigerator)
- Bowl of ice water

PREPARATION STEPS

1. Fill inner pot to just below maximum with hot water.
2. Select sous vide mode custom 75 °/c/167 °/f and set time for 30 minutes.
3. Place Hollandaise sauce ingredients into sous vide compatible zipper type bag, remove as much of the air as you can by lowering the bag into a bowl of water, using the water to push the air out of the bag, be careful not to allow any water into the bag. Seal while immersed or use a vacuum sealer.
4. Once up to temperature lower the bag into the Instant Pot. Close lid making sure pressure valve is open.
5. After 18 minutes open lid, gently lower egg(s) (unbroken, shell intact) into the water with a large, slotted spoon and close lid, making sure valve is open.
6. Once Instant Pot beeps, remove the eggs and place them in the ice water for one minute.
7. Gently break eggs and turn out.
8. Carefully remove hollandaise sauce and blend until smooth.
9. Spoon sauce onto eggs.
10. Perfect served with fresh buttered muffins on top of smoked bacon.

PREPARATION STEPS

1. Add 1 cup/250 ml of cold water plus the trivet to the pot, place egg(s) on the trivet.
2. Place the lid on the Instant Pot, set valve to seal, select manual high pressure (pressure cook custom high on Evo Plus) for 2 to 5 minutes (2 being very soft and 5 hard boiled) I think 3 minutes is perfect.
3. When Instant Pot beeps, quick release the pressure.
4. When pin drops open the lid. Press cancel.
5. If removing shells from the eggs and eating cold, leave them in ice water for 5 minutes first. If eating soft from an egg cup, place eggs point end down (to allow the larger area of white extra cooking time before you reach the bottom of the egg), eat immediately.

Tip: Boiled eggs are far easier to peel under a little running water.

Perfect Boiled Eggs

Perfect boiled eggs every time.

SERVES 1-6

INGREDIENTS

- 1-6 large eggs (from refrigerator)
- 1 cup/250 ml cold water for steaming
- Ice water

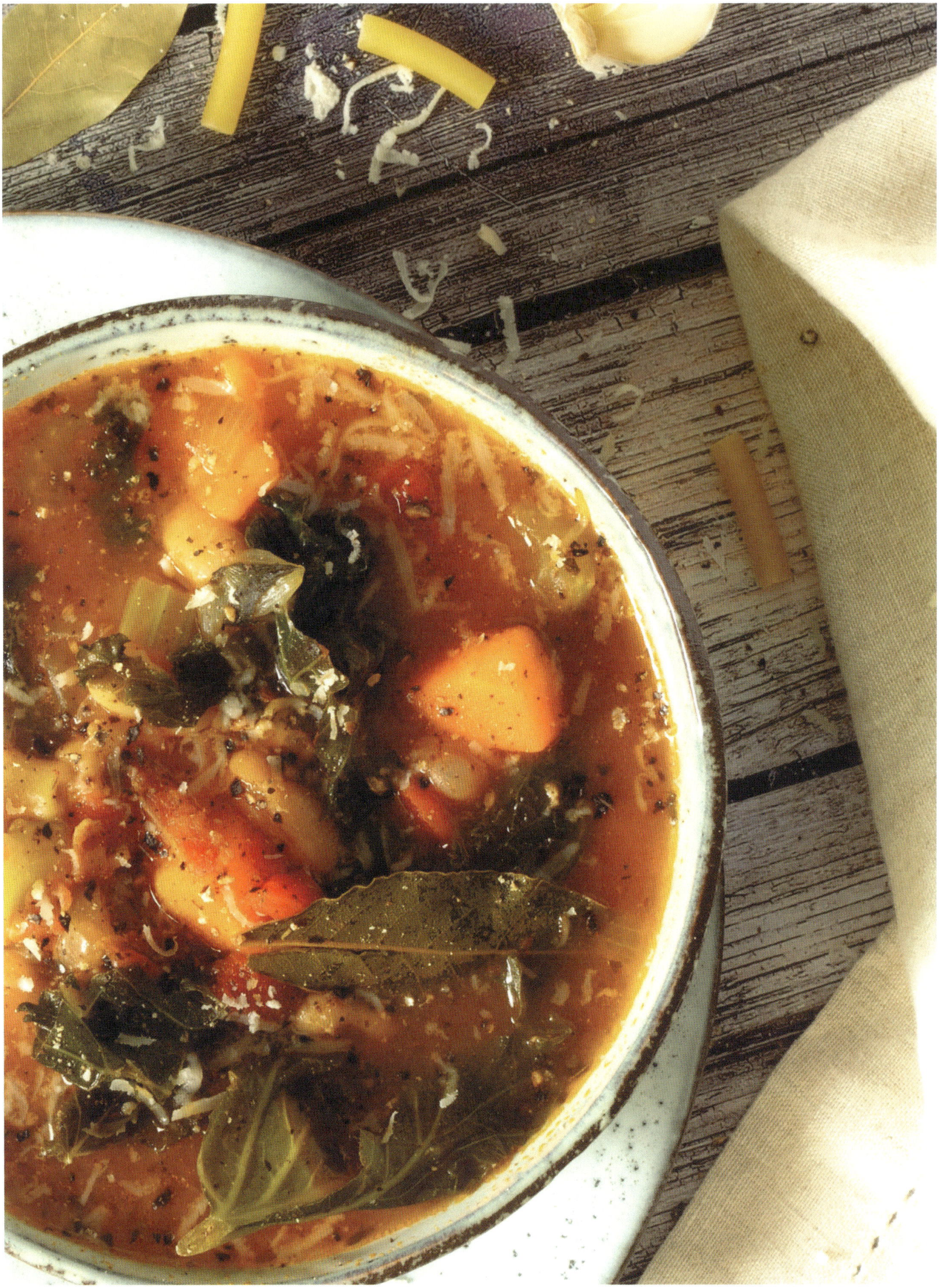

Soup

Scotch Broth

A hearty Scottish soup.

SERVES 4

INGREDIENTS

- 2 oz/60g chopped onions
- 1 peeled and crushed garlic clove
- 1 lb/450g zucchini/courgettes (cut in 1 inch/2.5 cm pieces)
- 2 cups/500 ml vegetable stock
- ½ tsp salt
- ¼ tsp ground white pepper
- 2 tsp/10g unsalted butter
- 3 tbsp/45g spreadable (cheese triangle type) cheese
- Salt and pepper to taste

PREPARATION STEPS

1. Add 2 oz/60g chopped onions, 1 peeled and crushed garlic clove, 1 lb/450g zucchini/courgettes (cut in 1 inch/2.5cm pieces), 2 cups/500 ml vegetable stock, ½ tsp salt and ¼ tsp ground white pepper to the Instant Pot.
2. Stir, then place the lid on the Instant Pot, set valve to seal, select manual high pressure (pressure cook custom high on Evo Plus) for 10 minutes.
3. When Instant Pot beeps, quick release the pressure.
4. When pin drops, open the lid.
5. Stir in 2 tsp/10g unsalted butter, and 3 tbsp/45g spreadable (cheese triangle type) cheese.
6. Pour into a blender in batches if necessary or blend straight in the pot with a heat resistant stick blender until desired consistency is achieved (If using a blender, ensure the blender is switched off first).
7. Add salt and pepper to taste, serve immediately.

Creamy Courgette/ Zucchini & Cheese soup

A beautifully tasty quick and easy to make soup.

SERVES 6

INGREDIENTS

- 2 oz/60g chopped onions
- 1 peeled and crushed garlic clove
- 1 lb/450g zucchini/courgettes (cut in 1 inch/2.5 cm pieces)
- 2 cups/500 ml vegetable stock. ½ tsp salt. ¼ tsp ground white pepper
- 2 tsp/10g unsalted butter
- 3 tbsp/45g spreadable (cheese triangle type) cheese
- Salt and pepper to taste

PREPARATION STEPS

1. Add 2 oz/60g chopped onions, 1 peeled and crushed garlic clovev, 1 lb/450g zucchini/courgettes (cut in 1 inch/2.5cm pieces), 2 cups/500 ml vegetable stock, ½ tsp salt and ¼ tsp ground white pepper to the Instant Pot.
2. Stir, then place the lid on the Instant Pot, set valve to seal, select manual high pressure (pressure cook custom high on Evo Plus) for 10 minutes.
3. When Instant Pot beeps, quick release the pressure.
4. When pin drops, open the lid.
5. Stir in 2 tsp/10g unsalted butter, and 3 tbsp/45g spreadable (cheese triangle type) cheese.
6. Pour into a blender in batches if necessary or blend straight in the pot with a heat resistant stick blender until desired consistency is achieved (If using a blender, ensure the blender is switched off first).
7. Add salt and pepper to taste, serve immediately.

Minestrone

A hearty Italian classic.

SERVES 4

INGREDIENTS

- 2 tbsp olive oil
- 4 rashers smoked streaky bacon (sliced)
- 1 garlic clove chopped)
- 2 medium white onions (½ inch/1 cm dice)
- 2 bay leaves
- ¼ tsp baking soda/sodium bicarbonate (not baking powder)
- 2 carrots (½ inch/1 cm dice)
- 2 celery sticks (½ inch/1 cm dice)
- 2 handfuls of seasonal greens (cabbage or kale, leaves shredded stalks finely chopped)
- 1 x 14 oz/400g can cannellini beans (undrained)
- 1 x 14 oz/400g can diced tomatoes
- 4 cups/1 litre vegetable stock
- ½ cup/100g macaroni
- 1 tsp Italian herbs
- ¼ tsp salt
- ¼ tsp black pepper
- Extra virgin olive oil and Parmesan cheese to serve

PREPARATION STEPS

1. Press the sauté button on the Instant Pot on normal heat, (custom level 3 for the Evo Plus) once display says HOT, add 2 tbsp of olive oil.

2. Add 4 rashers of smoked streaky bacon (sliced) to the Instant Pot, stir occasionally while you prepare your vegetables.

3. As soon as the bacon turns golden, add 1 garlic clove (chopped) and 2 medium onions (1/2 inch/1 cm dice) to the pot with the 2 bay leaves, stirring occasionally for a couple of minutes.

4. Add ¼ tsp baking soda, 2 carrots (½ inch/1 cm dice) and 2 celery sticks (½ inch/1 cm dice), cook for 5 minutes stirring regularly.

5. Add 2 handfuls of seasonal greens (cabbage or kale, leaves with stalks finely chopped), 1 x 14 oz/400g can cannellini beans (undrained), 1 x 14 oz/400g can of diced tomatoes, 4 cups/1 litre vegetable stock, ½ cup/100g dried macaroni, 1 tsp Italian herbs, ¼ tsp salt, and ¼ tsp black pepper.

6. Stir to mix everything, press cancel and place lid on Instant Pot, set valve to seal, select manual high pressure (pressure cook custom high on Evo Plus) for 4 minutes.

7. When Instant Pot beeps, quick release the pressure.

8. Season to taste then serve with a grating of parmesan cheese and a drizzle of extra virgin olive oil.

- 7 oz/200g canned chickpeas (drained and rinsed)
- 7 oz/200g canned lentils (drained and rinsed)
- 1 tbsp fresh chopped cilantro/coriander
- 2 tbsp fresh flatleaf parsley
- Lemon quarters to serve

PREPARATION STEPS

1. Peel 2 large ripe tomatoes by cutting a cross on the bottom of the tomatoes and then soaking them in boiling water for 30 seconds, the skin will then slide off easily.

2. Add 1 lb/450g cubed lamb, 1 medium onion (finely chopped), ½ tsp turmeric, ¼ tsp ground cinnamon, ¼ tsp ground ginger, ½ tsp paprika and 1 tbsp of the unsalted butter, 1 tsp salt and 2 cups cold water to the pot.

3. Place the lid on the Instant Pot, set valve to seal, select manual high pressure (pressure cook custom high on Evo Plus) for 15 minutes.

4. When Instant Pot beeps, allow 10 minutes before releasing the pressure.

5. When pin drops, open the lid.

6. Add 2 oz/50g long grain rice and 2 large ripe tomatoes (peeled and chopped) to the pot. Press cancel.

7. Place lid on Instant Pot, set valve to seal, select manual low pressure (pressure cook custom low on Evo Plus) for 6 minutes.

8. When Instant Pot beeps, allow 5 minutes before releasing the pressure.

9. Stir in the remaining butter, 7 oz/200g canned chickpeas (drained and rinsed) and 7 oz/200g canned lentils (drained and rinsed).

10. Select sauté as above, to warm through. Press cancel.

11. Check seasoning stir in 1 tbsp fresh chopped cilantro/coriander and 2 tbsp fresh flatleaf parsley.

12. Serve hot with lemon quarters.

Moroccan Harira Lamb

A traditional delicious and aromatic Moroccan soup.

SERVES 4

INGREDIENTS

- 1 lb/450g cubed lamb
- 1 medium onion (finely chopped)
- ½ tsp turmeric
- ¼ tsp ground cinnamon
- ¼ tsp ground ginger
- ½ tsp paprika
- 2 tbsp unsalted butter
- 1 tsp salt
- 2 cups cold water
- 2 oz/50g long grain rice
- 2 large ripe tomatoes (peeled and chopped)

Irish Leek & Potato Soup

A deliciously homely traditional Irish soup.

SERVES 6

INGREDIENTS

- 2 tbsp olive oil
- 2 tbsp unsalted butter
- 10 oz/300g leeks (washed, trimmed, and sliced)
- ½ tsp salt
- 9 oz/250g potatoes (peeled and 1 inch/2.5cm dice)
- 2 cups/500 ml vegetable stock
- 1 pinch of white pepper
- ¾ cup/180 ml of your preferred milk
- 1 pinch of ground nutmeg
- A handful of frozen peas for extra colour (optional)
- Fresh chives to garnish

PREPARATION STEPS

1. Press the sauté button on the Instant Pot on normal heat, (custom level 3 for the Evo Plus).
2. Once display says HOT, add 2 tbsp of olive oil and 2 tbsp unsalted butter, then add 10 oz/300g leeks (washed, trimmed, and sliced) and ½ tsp salt.
3. Sauté stirring regularly for 5 minutes.
4. Add 9 oz/250g potatoes (peeled and 1 inch/2.5cm dice), continue to cook for another 5 minutes stirring regularly.
5. Pour in 2 cups/500 ml vegetable stock and add 1 pinch of white pepper, stir and press cancel.
6. Place the lid on the Instant Pot, set valve to seal, select manual high pressure (pressure cook custom high on Evo Plus) for 10 minutes.
7. When Instant Pot beeps, quick release the pressure.
8. When pin drops, open the lid.
9. Stir in ¾ cup/180 ml of your preferred milk, 1 pinch of ground nutmeg and a handful of frozen peas for extra color (optional). Press cancel.
10. Pour into a blender in batches if necessary, alternatively blend straight in the pot with a heat resistant stick blender until desired consistency is achieved (If using a blender, ensure the blender is switched off first).
11. Serve hot, sprinkled with chopped fresh chives.

Vichyssoise (cold soup)

Allow soup to cool, then refrigerate for several hours. Adjust the seasoning to taste, serve cold with crusty bread.

- ½ medium onion (finely chopped)
- 8 oz/230g chestnut mushrooms (finely chopped)
- 1 x 14 oz/400g can green lentils (drained and rinsed)
- 1 medium carrot (⅓ inch/1 cm dice)
- 1 celery stick (⅓ inch/1 cm dice)
- 1 medium zucchini/courgette (1/3 inch/1 cm dice)
- 2 oz/50g green beans (trimmed and cut into ½ inch/1.5 cm pieces)
- 1 x 14 oz/400g can diced tomatoes
- 2 cups/500 ml vegetable stock

PREPARATION STEPS

1. Mix 1 ¼ tbsp Moroccan spice mix, ½ tsp allspice, 1 tsp cumin powder, 1 tsp paprika, ½ tsp freshly ground black pepper and ¼ tsp salt in a bowl. Reserve.

2. Press the sauté button on the Instant Pot on normal heat, (custom level 3 for the Evo Plus).

3. Once display says HOT, add 1 tbsp olive oil, 1 garlic clove (finely chopped) and ½ medium onion (finely chopped), cook for 2 minutes.

4. Add 8 oz/230g chestnut mushrooms (finely chopped) and the reserved spice mix, cook for 30 seconds stirring constantly.

5. Add 1 x 14 oz/400g can of green lentils (drained and rinsed), 1 medium carrot (1/3 inch/1 cm dice), 1 celery stick (1/3 inch/1 cm dice), 1 medium zucchini/courgette (1/3 inch/1 cm dice), 2 oz/50g green beans (trimmed and cut into ½ inch/1.5cm pieces), 1 x 14 oz/400g can of diced tomatoes and 2 cups/500 ml vegetable stock. Press cancel.

6. Place the lid on the Instant Pot, set valve to seal, select manual high pressure (pressure cook custom high on Evo Plus) for 5 minutes.

7. When Instant Pot beeps, allow 5 minutes before releasing the pressure.

8. When pin drops, open the lid.

9. Check seasoning.

10. Serve with Greek yogurt and fresh cilantro/coriander.

Moroccan Mushroom & Lentil Soup

A rich lentil soup loaded with vegetables & Moroccan spices.

SERVES 4

INGREDIENTS

- 1 ¼ tbsp Moroccan spice mix
- ½ tsp allspice
- 1 tsp cumin powder
- 1 tsp paprika
- ½ tsp freshly ground black pepper
- ¼ tsp salt
- 1 tbsp olive oil
- 1 garlic clove (finely chopped)

Mulligatawny

A spiced soup of South Indian origin.

___

SERVES 4

INGREDIENTS

- 2 tbsp olive oil
- 1 medium onion (finely chopped)
- 3 garlic cloves (finely chopped)
- 5 oz/150g carrot (diced ½ inch/1 cm)
- 5 oz/150g sweet potato (diced ½ inch/1 cm)
- 7 oz/200g green apples (diced ½ inch/1 cm)
- 2 tsp Madras curry powder
- 1 tsp ground cumin
- ½ tsp paprika
- ½ tsp ground cinnamon
- ½ tsp ground turmeric
- 1 tbsp tomato paste/puree
- ½ cup red split lentils (rinsed)
- 3 cups/750 ml vegetable stock
- 1 tsp salt
- ½ tsp freshly ground black pepper

PREPARATION STEPS

1. Press the sauté button on the Instant Pot on normal heat, (custom level 3 for the Evo Plus).

2. Once display says HOT add 2 tbsp of olive oil, 1 medium onion (finely chopped), 3 garlic cloves (finely chopped), 5 oz/150g carrot (diced ½ inch/1.5 cm), and 5 oz/150g sweet potato (diced ½ inch/1.5 cm). Sauté for 5 minutes stirring occasionally.

3. Add 7 oz/200g green apples (diced ½ inch/1.5 cm), 2 tsp Madras curry powder, 1 tsp ground cumin, ½ tsp paprika, ½ tsp ground cinnamon, and ½ tsp ground turmeric. Sauté for 30 seconds stirring constantly. Press cancel.

4. Stir in 1 tbsp tomato paste/puree, ½ cup red split lentils (rinsed), 3 cups/750 ml vegetable stock, 1 tsp salt, and ½ tsp freshly ground black pepper.

5. Place the lid on the Instant Pot, set valve to seal, select manual high pressure (pressure cook custom high on Evo Plus) for 5 minutes.

6. When Instant Pot beeps, allow 10 minutes before releasing the pressure.

7. When pin drops, open the lid and serve with sour cream.

Rice

Plain Rice

Sometimes you just need plain rice.

SERVES 4

INGREDIENTS

- 1 cup/180g of Basmati rice
- 1 ¼ cups/300 ml of cold water

PREPARATION STEPS

1. Rinse 1 cup/180g of Basmati rice in cold water, then soak in fresh cold water for 20 minutes, rinse a second time then drain in a colander.

2. Add rinsed Basmati rice and 1 ¼ cups/300 ml of cold water to the inner pot.

3. Place lid on Instant Pot, set valve to seal, select manual low pressure (pressure cook custom low on Evo Plus) for 6 minutes.

4. When Instant Pot beeps, quick release pressure.

5. Remove lid, cancel keep warm and remove inner pot to stop cooking process, gently fold rice with non-metallic spatula (to avoid breaking grains) and serve.

INGREDIENTS

- 1 cup/180g of Basmati rice
- 1 ¼ cups/300 ml of cold water
- 2 tsp ghee or vegetable oil
- ½ small white onion (finely diced)
- ½ tsp salt
- 6 green cardamom pods
- 4 cloves
- 2-inch cinnamon stick
- ½ tsp cumin seeds
- 2 bay leaves

PREPARATION STEPS

1. Rinse 1 cup/180g of Basmati rice in cold water, then soak in fresh cold water for 20 minutes, rinse a second time then drain in a colander.

2. Press the sauté button on the Instant Pot on normal heat, (custom level 3 for the Evo Plus) once display says HOT, add 2 tsp of ghee.

3. Once ghee is shimmering, add ½ a small white onion (finely diced), fry until the onion becomes translucent, then add 6 green cardamom pods, 4 cloves, 2 inch cinnamon stick, ½ tsp cumin seeds and 2 bay leaves and cook for one minute. Add 1 cup/180g of rice, stir to coat in the ghee then add 1 ¼ cups/300 ml of water and ½ tsp salt, give it another quick stir.

4. Press cancel, place lid on Instant Pot, set valve to seal, select manual low pressure (pressure cook custom low on Evo Plus) for 6 minutes.

5. When Instant Pot beeps, quick release pressure.

6. Remove lid, cancel keep warm and remove inner pot, to stop cooking process. Gently fold rice with non-metallic spatula (to avoid breaking grains) and serve.

Pilau

Probably the most ordered rice dish in Indian restaurants throughout the world.

A perfect companion to almost any Curry.

SERVES 4

Coconut Rice

Biryani inspired with caramelised onions stirred through and toasted coconut to complete.

SERVES 4

INGREDIENTS

- 1 cup of Basmati rice/180g
- 1 ¼ cups/300 ml of cold water
- 1 cup/240 ml of hot water (approx.)
- ½ cup/45g desiccated coconut
- 1 tbsp coconut oil
- One medium onion (thinly sliced)
- ½ tsp demerara sugar + extra for seasoning
- ½ tsp table salt + extra for seasoning

PREPARATION STEPS

1. Rinse 1 cup/180g of Basmati rice in cold water, then soak in fresh cold water for 20 minutes, rinse a second time then drain in a colander.

2. Press the sauté button on the Instant Pot on normal heat, (custom level 3 for the Evo Plus) once display says HOT, add ½ cup/45g of desiccated coconut, stirring continuously for about 20 seconds or until the grains start to brown, then pour onto a plate to cool.

3. Place inner pot back into Instant Pot whilst still in sauté mode, heat 1 tbsp coconut oil then add the onion, ¼ tsp of the salt and ¼ tsp of the sugar. Keep the onions moving for about 2 minutes or until they just start to brown. Add approximately ¼ cup of the hot water at a time, the idea is to steam and sauté them. Place a large plate or a lid on the pot to slow down evaporation and allow them to soften. If you have an Instant Pot glass lid now is the time to use it. Keep checking, stirring, and adding water as it evaporates. When they are golden brown, and all water has evaporated, remove them from the pot and set aside for later.

4. Add drained rice to the pot, give it a stir to coat with residue then add 1 ¼ cold water and ¼ tsp of the salt and ¼ tsp of the sugar and give it another stir.

5. Press cancel, place lid on Instant Pot, set valve to seal, select manual low pressure (pressure cook custom low on Evo Plus) for 6 minutes.

6. When Instant Pot beeps, quick release pressure.

7. Remove lid, cancel keep warm and remove inner pot to stop cooking process, add the coconut, then the reserved onion a little at a time, gently stirring with a non-metallic spatula (to avoid breaking grains). Season if required and serve.

Spiced Mexican Rice

An excellent accompaniment to many Mexican dishes.

SERVES 4

INGREDIENTS

- 1 cup/180g of Basmati rice
- 1 ¼ cups/300 ml of cold water (plain rice recipe)
- 1 medium red onion (finely chopped)
- 1 red pepper (finely chopped)
- ¼ cup/60g canned kidney beans (drained and rinsed)
- 2 tbsp canned sweetcorn
- 2 garlic cloves ((finely chopped)
- 2 tomatoes (finely chopped)
- ¼ cup/60g jarred jalapeno peppers (finely chopped)
- 1 tsp cumin powder
- ½ tsp turmeric powder
- ½ tsp salt
- Pinch of sugar
- ½ tsp dried oregano
- Pinch of smoked paprika
- 2 tbsp olive oil
- Cilantro/coriander leaves to garnish

PREPARATION STEPS

1. In a large bowl, mix 1 medium red onion (finely chopped), 1 red pepper (finely chopped), ¼ cup/60g canned kidney beans (drained and rinsed), 2 tbsp canned sweetcorn, 2 garlic cloves (finely chopped), 2 tomatoes (finely chopped) and ¼ cup/60g of jarred jalapeno peppers (finely chopped). Set aside.

2. In a separate bowl, combine 1 tsp cumin powder, ½ tsp turmeric powder, ½ tsp salt, pinch of sugar, ½ tsp dried oregano, and a pinch of smoked paprika. Set aside.

3. Press the sauté button on the Instant Pot on normal heat, (custom level 3 for the Evo Plus).

4. Once display says HOT add 2 tbsp of olive oil.

5. Add the vegetables and sauté for 6-7 minutes, stirring regularly.

6. Add the spices and continue to cook for another minute.

7. Add the precooked rice and cook for a further 3 minutes, stirring regularly until rice is heated through.

8. Serve with fresh cilantro/coriander leaves to garnish.

Chicken & Chorizo Risotto

The perfect risotto without having to stand and stir.

SERVES 4

INGREDIENTS

- 1 tbsp olive oil
- 1 onion (finely chopped)
- 2 garlic cloves (crushed)
- ½ cup/80g sliced chorizo
- 1 cup/130g sliced mushrooms
- 1 red bell pepper (diced)
- 1 lb/450g skinless boneless chicken thighs (sliced)
- ½ tsp smoked paprika
- ½ tsp salt
- 2/3 cup/150 ml white wine
- 2 ½ cups/600 ml cold water
- 1 & 2/3 cups 300g arborio/risotto rice
- 1 tsp vegetable bouillon
- 1 tbsp unsalted butter
- Grated Parmesan
- Freshly ground black pepper
- 4 sliced green onions/spring onions

PREPARATION STEPS

1. Press the sauté button on the Instant Pot on normal heat, (custom level 3 for the Evo Plus)
2. Once display says HOT, add 1 tbsp of the olive oil, 1 onion (finely chopped), 2 garlic cloves (crushed), ½ cup/80g sliced chorizo, 1 cup/130g sliced mushrooms, 1 red bell pepper (diced), 1 lb/450g skinless boneless chicken thighs (sliced), ½ tsp smoked paprika and ½ tsp salt.
3. Sauté for 5 minutes.
4. Add 2/3 cup/150 ml white wine, stir to deglaze the pot for a couple of minutes.
5. Add 2 ½ cups/600 ml cold water, 1 & 2/3 cups 300g arborio/risotto rice and 1 tsp vegetable bouillon, stir well.
6. Place the lid on the Instant Pot, set valve to seal, select manual low pressure (pressure cook custom low on Evo Plus) for 12 minutes.
7. When Instant Pot beeps, quick release the pressure.
8. When pin drops, open the lid.
9. Stir well until creamy then stir in 1 tbsp unsalted butter.
10. Let stand for three minutes.
11. Serve with grated Parmesan, both stirred in and sprinkled on, along with freshly ground black pepper and 4 sliced green onions/spring onions.

Whole Spices

- 6 cardamom pods
- 1 tsp cumin seeds
- 2 bay leaves
- 2-inch cinnamon stick
- ½ tsp fennel seeds
- 4 cloves
- ½ tsp freshly ground black pepper
- ½ tsp salt

Other Ingredients

- 3 tbsp vegetable oil
- 2 red onions (finely sliced)
- Fresh ginger (thumb sized finely chopped)
- 2 cloves of garlic (finely chopped)
- 1 green chilli (sliced)
- 2 medium tomatoes (sliced)
- 1 cup of small cauliflower florets
- 1 cup of carrots (1 cm slice)
- 1 cup of new potatoes (1 cm slice, skin on)
- ¼ cup of French beans (roughly chopped
- 1 tsp chilli powder
- ½ tsp turmeric powder
- 2 tsp garam masala
- 1 tsp coriander powder
- ½ cup of full fat Greek yogurt
- ½ cup of fresh mint leaves
- ½ cup fresh coriander leaves
- ½ tsp salt
- 2 cups of Basmati rice
- 2 ½ cup of hot water
- 1 pinch of saffron

PREPARATION STEPS

1. Press the sauté button on the Instant Pot on normal heat, (custom level 3 for the Evo Plus) once display says HOT, heat 2 tbsp vegetable oil, add 2 medium onions, ½ tsp of salt and ½ tsp of light brown sugar.
2. Keep the onions moving for about 2 minutes or until they just start to brown. Add approximately ¼ cup of the hot water at a time, the idea is to steam and sauté them. Place a large plate or a lid on the pot to slow down evaporation and allow them to soften. If you have an Instant Pot glass lid now is the time to use it. Keep checking, stirring, and adding water as it

Vegetable Biryani

Long grained rice, richly flavoured with exotic spices, layered with fresh vegetables.

Who can resist?

SERVES 8

INGREDIENTS

For Caramelised Onions

- 2 tbsp vegetable oil
- 2 medium onions (thinly sliced)
- ½ tsp table salt
- ½ tsp light brown sugar
- 1 cup (approx.) of hot water

evaporates. When the onions are golden brown, and all water has evaporated, remove them from the pot and set aside for later.

3. Still on sauté mode, when display says HOT, add 3 tbsp vegetable oil, 2 red onions (finely sliced), all the whole spices, fresh ginger (thumb sized finely chopped), 2 cloves of garlic (finely chopped), 1 green chilli (sliced), and ½ tsp salt.
4. Sauté, stirring regularly until onions start to turn golden.
5. Stir in 2 medium tomatoes (sliced), 1 cup of small cauliflower florets, 1 cup of carrots (1 cm slice), 1 cup of new potatoes (1 cm slice, skin on), ¼ cup of French beans (roughly chopped, 1 tsp chilli powder, ½ tsp turmeric powder, 2 tsp garam masala, and 1 tsp coriander powder.
6. Sauté for 1 minute.
7. Add ½ cup of hot water and mix.
8. Press cancel, place lid on Instant Pot, set valve to seal, select manual high pressure (pressure cook custom high on Evo Plus) for 5 minutes.
9. Rinse 2 cups of Basmati rice in cold water, and then soak for 20 minutes in fresh water, rinse a second time then drain in colander.
10. Soak the saffron in ¼ cup of boiling water.
11. When the Instant Pot beeps, allow 5 minutes natural pressure release, then quick release.
12. Press cancel, stir in ½ cup of full fat Greek yogurt, add ½ the rice to the pot, 1/3 of the caramelised onions, and 1/3 of the fresh mint and coriander leaves. Add a second layer of the rice, ½ tsp of table salt, and another third of the caramelised onions. Sprinkle the saffron water over the rice and add another 1/3 of the mint and coriander leaves.
13. Add remaining 2 cups of hot water from the side of the pot, to avoid disturbing the contents, or however much it takes to just cover the rice.
14. Place the lid on the Instant Pot, set valve to seal, select manual low pressure (pressure cook low on Evo Plus) for 6 minutes.
15. When the Instant Pot beeps, quick release the pressure.
16. Add remaining mint coriander and onions as a garnish.
17. Fluff up rice and serve.

PREPARATION STEPS

1. Rinse 1 cup/180g of Basmati rice in cold water, then soak in fresh cold water for 20 minutes, rinse a second time then drain in a colander.

2. Add 1 cup of rice and 1 ¼ cups/300 ml cold water to the Instant Pot, place lid on, set valve to seal, select manual low pressure (pressure cook custom low on Evo Plus) for 6 minutes.

3. When Instant Pot beeps, quick release pressure.

4. Remove lid, cancel keep warm and remove inner pot, to stop cooking process. Gently fold rice a few times with non-metallic spatula (to avoid breaking grains) for a couple of minutes.

5. Remove from pot and allow to cool a little.

6. For the next step it's your choice whether to use a large pan on a medium heat, or your Instant Pot on sauté, normal heat, (custom level 3 for the Evo Plus).

7. Add 1 tbsp of stir fry oil, when hot add 5oz/150g of bacon lardons 1 med white onion and 2 cloves of finely chopped garlic, and sauté stirring often until onions just start to brown slightly.

8. Add 1 cup of vegetables, sauté for 2 minutes.

9. Add ¼ tsp of the sesame oil to the 2 beaten eggs, push the contents of the pan to one side and pour in the egg mixture half at a time to scramble without flooding the pan.

10. Stir in as much rice as you want to add, you don't need to use all of it, it's your preference, add 5 and 7 spice to your taste.

11. Add the remainder of the sesame oil.

12. Cook for 4 minutes turning regularly.

13. add 3 green/spring onions (sliced) and cook for another minute.

14. Enjoy.

Egg Fried Rice

This has always been my most popular rice dish amongst my kids.

SERVES 4

INGREDIENTS

- 1 cup/180g of Basmati rice
- 1 ¼ cups/300 ml cold water
- 1 tbsp stir fry oil
- 5 oz/150g smoked bacon lardons
- 1 medium white onion (chopped)
- 2 cloves garlic (finely chopped)
- 1 cup of finely chopped vegetables of your choice
- 2 large eggs (beaten)
- Chinese 5 spice (to taste)
- 1 ¼ tsp sesame oil
- 3 green/spring onions (sliced)

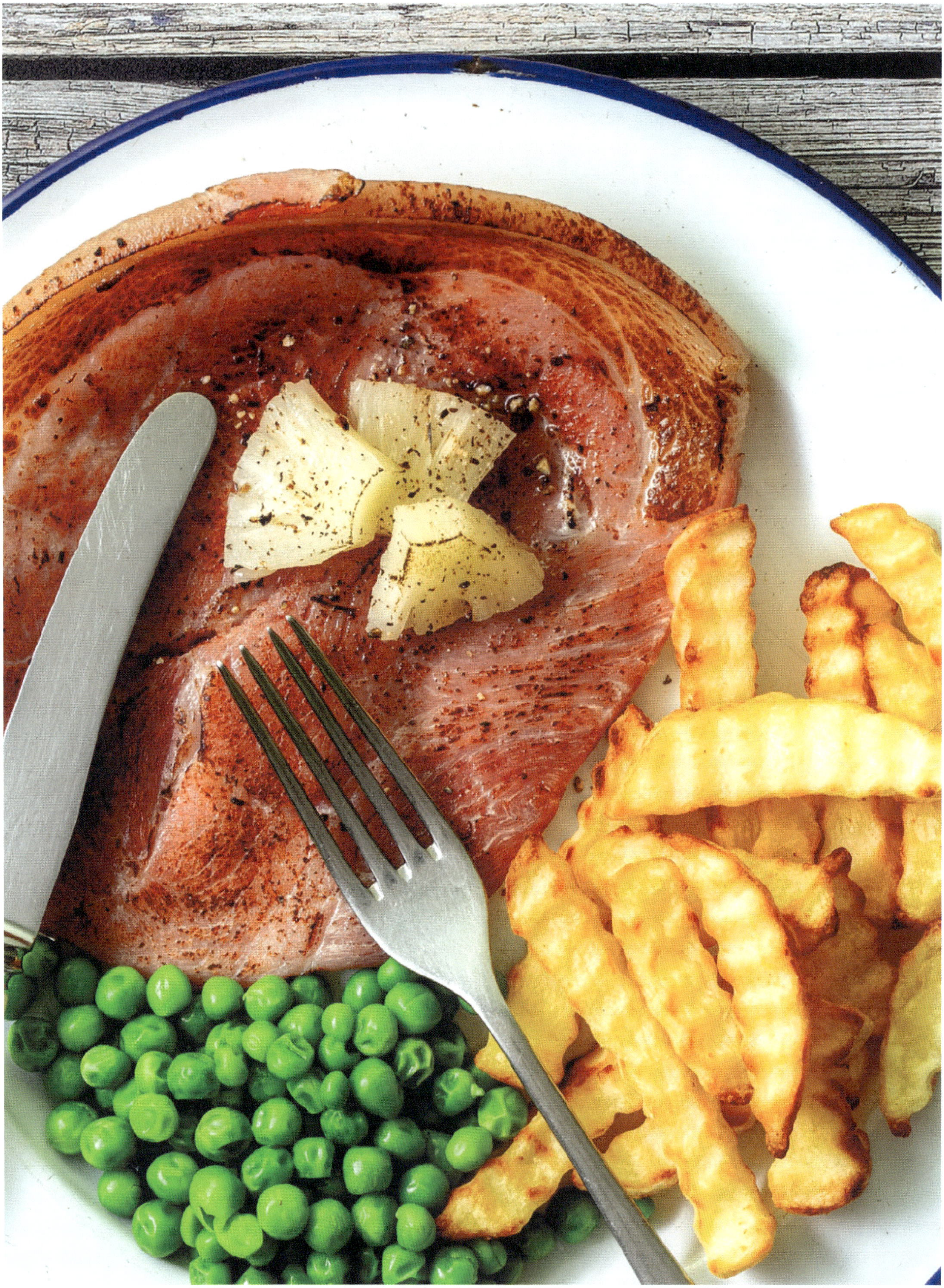

Pork

Slow Cooked Pork & Pineapple Curry

A nice combination of savoury, sweetness, and heat, perfect to come home to.

SERVES 4

INGREDIENTS

- 1 cup/180g of Basmati rice
- 1 ¼ cups/300 ml cold water
- 1 tbsp stir fry oil
- 5 oz/150g smoked bacon lardons
- 1 medium white onion (chopped)
- 2 cloves garlic (finely chopped)
- 1 cup of finely chopped vegetables of your choice
- 2 large eggs (beaten)
- Chinese 5 spice (to taste)
- 1 ¼ tsp sesame oil
- 3 green/spring onions (sliced)

PREPARATION STEPS

1. Mix 3 tbsp plain/all-purpose flour with 1 tsp salt, toss 2 ¼lb/1kg lean cubed pork into mixture until coated.
2. Press the sauté button on the Instant Pot on normal heat, (custom level 3 for the Evo Plus) once display says HOT, add 2 tbsp of the olive oil.
3. Brown meat on all sides, then set aside.
4. Add the 2 remaining tbsp of olive oil to the pot, and 1 onion (finely chopped), sauté until transparent.
5. Add the browned pork back to the pot and all remaining ingredients, bring to a boil.
6. Press cancel and place the lid on the Instant Pot.
7. Make sure valve is NOT set to seal.
8. Press the slow cook button on the Instant Pot, press adjust to less, and + or – to 8 hours.
9. On the Evo Plus press slow cook/custom/8 hours/low/start.
10. After 8 hours the Instant Pot will automatically go into keep warm mode.
11. Press cancel, discard bay leaves, and stir well.
12. Serve with rice.

PREPARATION STEPS

1. Press the sauté button on the Instant Pot on normal heat, (custom level 3 for the Evo Plus) once display says HOT, heat 1 tbsp of the oil.
2. Sauté 12 good quality pork sausages, turning regularly until nicely browned, set to one side.
3. Add 2 tablespoons of the olive oil, 2 thinly sliced red onions, 3 crushed cloves of garlic and ¼ tsp table salt.
4. Sauté stirring regularly until the onions start to brown, then add 2 tbsp balsamic vinegar and 1 tsp Worcestershire sauce.
5. Reduce for 1 minute.
6. Add ¾ cup/180 ml of beef stock, and ½ cup/125 ml of passata/tomato puree, bring to a boil.
7. Press cancel and add sausages. Place lid on Instant Pot, set valve to seal, select manual high pressure (pressure cook custom high on Evo Plus) for 10 minutes.
8. When Instant Pot beeps, allow 10 minutes natural pressure release, then open the valve to release the rest of the pressure.
9. When pin drops, open the lid.
10. Best served with mashed potatoes and fresh vegetables.

Sausages in Balsamic Onion Gravy

Packed with flavour from a balsamic reduction.

SERVES 4

INGREDIENTS

- 3 tbsp olive oil
- 12 good quality pork sausages
- 2 medium sized red onions (thinly sliced)
- 3 garlic cloves (crushed)
- ¼ tsp table salt
- 2 tbsp balsamic vinegar
- 1 tsp Worcestershire sauce
- ¾ cup/180 ml beef stock
- ½ cup/125 ml passata/tomato puree

Sweet & Sour Pork with Peppers

Easy and tasty.
No need for a takeout.

SERVES 4

INGREDIENTS

- 1 x 14 oz/400g can of pineapple chunks
- ¼ cup/60 ml of white vinegar
- 2 tbsp light soy sauce
- 1½ tsp salt
- ¼ tsp ginger powder
- 1 lb/450g boneless pork loin (cut into 1-inch pieces)
- 1 large onion (cut into chunks)
- 1 green and 1 red bell pepper (cut into chunks)
- 2 tbsp cornflour/cornstarch
- 2 tbsp water

PREPARATION STEPS

1. Add the juice/syrup from 1 x 14 oz/400 g can of pineapple chunks into the Instant Pot. Set aside the pineapple for later.

2. Stir in ¼ cup/60 ml of white vinegar, 2 tbsp light soy sauce, 1½ tsp salt, ¼ tsp ginger powder, and 1 lb/450g boneless pork loin (cut into 1-inch pieces).

3. Place lid on Instant Pot, set valve to seal, select manual high pressure (pressure cook custom high on Evo Plus) for 5 minutes.

4. When Instant Pot beeps, allow 10 minutes natural pressure release, then open the valve to release the rest of the pressure.

5. Add 1 large onion (cut into chunks), 1 green and 1 red bell pepper (cut into chunks) and the reserved pineapple. Press cancel.

6. Select sauté on the Instant Pot on normal heat, (custom level 3 for the Evo Plus).

7. Simmer stirring occasionally for 5 minutes, or until onions and peppers are just tender.

8. Mix 2 tbsp of cornflour/cornstarch, with 2 tbsp of cold water.

9. Stir the cornflour/cornstarch slurry a little at a time into the sauce until desired thickness is achieved, continue cooking for another 30 seconds until the sauce is smooth. Press cancel.

10. Perfect served with rice.

INGREDIENTS

- 1 lb/450g lean sliced pork loin
- 1 tbsp seasoned all-purpose/plain flour
- 2 tbsp olive oil
- 1 onion (sliced)
- 1 apple (skin on, cored and cut into thin wedges)
- ¾ cup/180 ml vegetable or chicken stock
- 2 bay leaves
- 1 tbsp wholegrain mustard
- 2 tbsp chopped flatleaf parsley
- Salt and freshly ground black pepper (to taste)

PREPARATION STEPS

1. Coat 1 lb/450g lean sliced diced pork loin, with 1 tbsp seasoned all-purpose/plain flour.
2. Press the sauté button on the Instant Pot on normal heat, (custom level 3 for the Evo Plus).
3. Once display says HOT, add 1 tbsp of the olive oil
4. Brown meat on all sides and set aside. Deglaze the pot with a little hot water.
5. Add the 1 remaining tbsp of olive oil to the pot, and 1 onion (sliced), sauté stirring occasionally until brown.
6. Add 1 apple (skin on, cored and cut into thin wedges), sauté until it has slightly caramelised.
7. Stir in ¾ cup/180 ml vegetable or chicken stock, de glazing with a wooden spatula any bits from the bottom of the pot. Press cancel. (dissolving this sediment into our stock adds lots of flavour).
8. Return the pork to the pot, add 2 bay leaves, 1 tbsp wholegrain mustard and stir.
9. Place the lid on the Instant Pot, set valve to seal, select manual low pressure (pressure cook custom low on Evo Plus) for 5 minutes.
10. When Instant Pot beeps, allow 5 minutes before releasing the pressure.
11. When pin drops, open the lid.
12. Stir in 2 tbsp chopped flatleaf parsley, add salt and freshly ground black pepper to taste before serving.

Braised Pork & Apple

A low fat one pot dish that's perfect for a family supper.

Serve with bread or potatoes and your preferred vegetables.

SERVES 4

Ham, Beans & Orange

Comforting fresh and simple.

SERVES 4

INGREDIENTS

- ½ orange
- 2 tbsp olive oil
- 1 large onion (chopped)
- 2 celery stalks (chopped)
- 1 lb/450g piece of Virginia ham/gammon (cut into 1.5 inch/4 cm chunks)
- 1 tbsp paprika
- 3 tbsp dark muscovado sugar
- 1 tbsp black treacle or molasses
- 2 tbsp white wine vinegar
- 3 tbsp tomato paste/puree
- 4 cloves
- 1 cup/240 ml chicken stock
- 2 x 14 oz/400g haricot beans (drained and rinsed)
- Salt and black pepper to taste

PREPARATION STEPS

1. Grate the zest from ½ orange and set aside, reserve the orange flesh for later.

2. Press the sauté button on the Instant Pot on normal heat, (custom level 3 for the Evo Plus).

3. Once display says HOT, add 2 tbsp of olive oil.

4. Add 1 large onion (chopped), and 2 celery stalks (chopped), sauté for about 8 minutes stirring occasionally, until golden.

5. Add 1 lb/450g piece of Virginia ham/gammon (cut into 1.5 inch/4 cm chunks), and 1 tbsp paprika.

6. Stir for 1 minute.

7. Add orange zest, 3 tbsp dark muscovado sugar, 1 tbsp black treacle or molasses, 2 tbsp white wine vinegar, 2-3 tbsp tomato paste/puree, and 4 cloves. Stir well.

8. Press cancel. Pour in 1 cup/240 ml chicken stock.

9. Place the lid on the Instant Pot, set valve to seal, select manual high pressure (pressure cook custom high on Evo Plus) for 15 minutes.

10. When Instant Pot beeps, allow 10 minutes before releasing the pressure.

11. When pin drops, open the lid.

12. Press cancel, then press sauté (normal setting as earlier).

13. Stir in 2 x 14 oz/400g of haricot beans (drained and rinsed).

14. Peel the orange (cutting away all the white) and cut into chunks. Stir into the pot and check for seasoning.

15. Garnish with green/spring onions and grated cheese.

Pork with Tomato & Fennel

Subtle, sweet, and low fat.

SERVES 4

INGREDIENTS

- 2 tbsp olive oil
- 1 lb/450g lean sliced pork loin
- 1 large onion (sliced)
- 3 garlic cloves (crushed)
- 2 x 14 oz/400g can chopped tomatoes
- 2 tbsp tomato paste/puree
- ½ tsp caster sugar
- 1 tsp vegetable bouillon or 1 vegetable stock cube
- 1 tsp salt and ¼ tsp freshly ground black pepper
- 1 large fennel bulb (sliced)
- Grated zest of 1 lemon

PREPARATION STEPS

1. Press the sauté button on the Instant Pot on normal heat, (custom level 3 for the Evo Plus).
2. Once display says HOT, add 1 tbsp of the olive oil
3. Brown 1lb/450g lean sliced pork loin on all sides, then set to one side.
4. Add the 1 remaining tbsp of olive oil to the pot, 1 onion (sliced), and 3 garlic cloves (crushed), sauté stirring occasionally until golden.
5. Stir in 2 x 14 oz/400g can chopped tomatoes, 2 tbsp tomato paste/puree, ½ tsp caster sugar, 1 tsp vegetable bouillon or 1 vegetable stock cube, then add the reserved pork.
6. Season with 1 tsp salt and ¼ tsp freshly ground pepper.
7. Trim the fronds from the fennel, roughly chop and set aside. Thinly slice the bulb and stir into the pot. Press cancel.
8. Place the lid on the Instant Pot, set valve to seal, select manual high pressure (pressure cook custom high on Evo Plus) for 10 minutes.
9. When Instant Pot beeps, allow 10 minutes before releasing the pressure.
10. When pin drops, open the lid.
11. Check seasoning.
12. Stir in the grated zest of 1 lemon, garnish with the chopped fennel fronds, then serve.

Pork & Celeriac

Melt in the mouth pork in a tangy sauce.

SERVES 4

INGREDIENTS

- 1 lb/450g boneless pork shoulder (cut into bite sized chunks)
- Salt and freshly ground black pepper (to season pork)
- 2 tbsp olive oil
- 2 tsp unsalted butter
- 1 lb/450g celeriac (peeled and chopped into large chunks)
- 2 leeks (trimmed and sliced)
- 2 medium carrots (peeled and chopped into chunks)
- 2 garlic cloves (crushed)
- ¼ tsp baking soda/sodium bicarbonate (not baking powder)
- ½ cup/125 ml dry white wine
- ½ cup/125 ml chicken or vegetable stock
- 1 tbsp soy sauce
- Finely grated zest and juice of half a medium orange
- 1 large rosemary sprig
- 1 ½ tbsp cornstarch/cornflour
- 1 ½ tbsp cold water

PREPARATION STEPS

1. Press the sauté button on the Instant Pot on normal heat, (custom level 3 for the Evo Plus).
2. Season 1 lb/450g boneless pork shoulder (cut into bite sized chunks), with salt and freshly ground black pepper.
3. Once display says HOT, add 1 tbsp of the olive oil, and 1 tsp of the unsalted butter.
4. Sauté the pork until browned, remove from the pot.
5. Add the remainder of the olive oil and butter, sauté 1 lb/450g celeriac (peeled and chopped into large chunks), 2 leeks (trimmed and sliced). 2 medium carrots (peeled and chopped into chunks), 2 garlic cloves (crushed) and ¼ tsp baking soda/sodium bicarbonate (not baking powder), for 5 minutes until it starts to soften.
6. Add the reserved pork and its juices back to the pot, with ½ cup/125 ml dry white wine, ½ cup/125 ml chicken or vegetable stock, 1 tbsp soy sauce, finely grated zest, the juice of half a medium orange, and 1 large rosemary sprig.
7. Place the lid on the Instant Pot, set valve to seal, select manual high pressure (pressure cook custom high on Evo Plus) for 15 minutes.
8. When Instant Pot beeps, allow 10 minutes before releasing the pressure.
9. When pin drops, open the lid.
10. Check seasoning. Press sauté, on normal heat, while mixing in 1 ½ tbsp cornstarch/cornflour with 1½ tbsp cold water, stir in to thicken. Press cancel.

Pineapple Infused Sous Vide Gammon Steaks

Sweet pineapple and seared gammon… perfection.

SERVES 4

INGREDIENTS

- 4 good quality smoked Virginia ham/gammon steaks (fat on, approx ½ inch/1.3 cm thick)
- 1 x 7 oz/200g can pineapple chunks
- 1 tbsp cornstarch/cornflour
- 1 tbsp cold water

PREPARATION STEPS

1. Fill inner pot to ¾ full with hot water. Select sous vide mode custom 65 °/c/150 °/f, set time for 3 hours, and bring up to temperature.

2. In 2 sous vide compatible zipper type bags, place 2 Virginia ham/gammon steaks in each bag. Drain and refrigerate 1 x 7 oz/200g can of pineapple chunks, divide the juice between the 2 bags.

3. Remove as much of the air as you can by lowering the bags into a bowl of water, using the water to push the air out of the bag, being careful not to allow any water into the bag. Seal while immersed or use a vacuum sealer.

4. Once up to temperature, cook for 3 hours.

5. Once cooked, pour out the juice from the bags into a small pan, add reserved pineapple chunks and reduce, adding a little of the 1 tbsp cornstarch/cornflour and 1 tbsp cold water slurry, to thicken slightly. Keep warm.

6. Remove the steaks from the bags, pat dry with kitchen towel. In a safe place on a wire rack, using a kitchen blowtorch, sear the steak until golden brown, or apply a little high smoke point cooking oil to them, then sear quickly (to avoid cooking through) on both sides in a very hot preheated preferably heavy gauge pan.

7. Pour the sauce over the steaks, enjoy with fries and peas.

Shredded Pork & Cider Rolls

Best served with apple sauce.

SERVES 4

INGREDIENTS

- 1 lb/450g pork tenderloin (cut in half, with the sinew cut away)
- ¾ cup/180 ml dry cider
- 1 medium onion (finely chopped)
- 1 garlic clove (finely chopped)
- 1 tbsp Dijon mustard
- 1 tbsp dark brown sugar
- 1 tsp salt
- ½ tsp freshly ground black pepper
- 2 tbsp unsalted butter
- 3 sprigs fresh tarragon (leaves only)
- 8 bread rolls
- Apple sauce (to serve)

PREPARATION STEPS

1. Add 1 lb/450g pork tenderloin (cut in half with the sinew cut away), and ¾ cup/180 ml dry cider, to the inner pot.

2. Place the lid on the Instant Pot, set valve to seal, select manual high pressure (pressure cook custom high on Evo Plus) for 30 minutes.

3. When Instant Pot beeps, allow 10 minutes before releasing the pressure.

4. When pin drops, open the lid. Press cancel.

5. Remove pork onto a platter, pull apart with 2 forks. Reserve the liquid in the inner pot.

6. Place the shredded pork, 1 medium onion (finely chopped), 1 garlic clove (finely chopped), 1 tbsp Dijon mustard, 1 tbsp dark brown sugar, 1 tsp salt, ½ tsp freshly ground black pepper, 2 tbsp unsalted butter and 3 sprigs fresh tarragon (leaves only), to the inner pot containing the reserved liquid.

7. Press the sauté button on the Instant Pot on normal heat, (custom level 3 for the Evo Plus).

8. Cook for 10 minutes, stirring occasionally.

9. Mix the pork back into the sauce.

10. Serve with apple sauce.

Lamb

Braised Lamb Shoulder

Beautiful fall off the bone braised lamb, cooked in little more than an hour.

SERVES 4

INGREDIENTS

- 14 flu oz/400 ml lamb stock from granules or stock cubes
- 1.6 lb/750g leg or shoulder (bone in preferably)
- 1.4 oz/40g dried pearl barley
- 7 oz/200g baby potatoes (1.5 inches/ 4 cm)
- 7 oz/200g carrots (peeled and sliced 1.5 inches/4 cm)
- 2 celery sticks sliced 1.5 inches/4 cm
- 1 leek (trimmed and sliced 1 inch/2 cm)
- 5 oz/150g shallots (whole, peeled)
- ½ tsp salt
- 2 tbsp cornflour/cornstarch mixed with 2 tbsp water
- 3.5 oz/100g frozen peas (defrosted)
- ½ tsp mint sauce

PREPARATION STEPS

1. Add 14 flu oz/400ml lamb stock from granules or cubes, and 1.6 lb/750g leg or shoulder (bone in preferably) to the Instant Pot.

2. Place lid on Instant Pot, set valve to seal, select manual high pressure (pressure cook custom high on Evo Plus) for 20 minutes.

3. When Instant Pot beeps, allow 10 minutes natural pressure release, then open the valve to release the rest of the pressure.

4. When pin drops, open the lid.

5. Stir in 1.4 oz/40g dried pearl barley. 7 oz/200g baby potatoes (1.5 inches/4 cm), 7 oz/200g carrots (peeled and sliced 1.5 inches/4 cm), 2 celery sticks sliced 1.5 inches/4 cm, 1 leek trimmed and sliced 1 inch/2 cm. 5 oz/150g shallots (whole, peeled), and ½ tsp salt.

6. Place lid on Instant Pot, set valve to seal, select manual high pressure (pressure cook custom high on Evo Plus) for 20 minutes.

7. When Instant Pot beeps, allow 10 minutes natural pressure release, open the valve to release the rest of the pressure.

8. When pin drops, open the lid.

9. Press the sauté button on the Instant Pot on normal heat, (custom level 3 for the Evo Plus).

10. Gradually pour in the cornflour/cornstarch slurry (stirring carefully so as not to break up the soft vegetables) until desired thickness is achieved. Press cancel.

11. Add 3.5 oz/100g frozen peas (defrosted), and ½ tsp of mint sauce.

12. Carefully stir in. Serve with fresh crusty bread.

PREPARATION STEPS

1. Add to the pot, 1 lb/450g lamb (cubed), 1 x 14 oz/400g can of chopped tomatoes, 1 tbsp harissa paste, ½ tsp salt, and ¼ tsp freshly ground black pepper.
2. Stir, then place the lid on the Instant Pot, set valve to seal, select manual high pressure (pressure cook custom high on Evo Plus) for 20 minutes.
3. When Instant Pot beeps, allow 10 minutes before releasing the pressure.
4. When pin drops, open the lid. Press cancel.
5. Remove excess oil from the surface by blotting with kitchen towel.
6. Stir in 1 x 14 oz/400g can chickpeas (drained and rinsed).
7. Check seasoning, adding more salt, pepper or harissa paste if needed.
8. Serve with rice, yoghurt, and scattered cilantro/coriander.

Spiced Lamb with Tomato & Chickpeas

A very tasty dish, ideal if you're short on time.

SERVES 4

INGREDIENTS

- 1 lb/450g lamb (cubed)
- 1 x 14 oz/400g can chopped tomatoes
- 2 tbsp harissa paste
- ½ tsp salt
- ½ tsp freshly ground black pepper
- 1 x 14 oz/400g can chickpeas (drained and rinsed)
- Large handful of roughly chopped fresh cilantro/coriander

Moussaka

A pressure cooked version of the classic Greek dish.

SERVES 4

INGREDIENTS

- 1 tbsp olive oil
- 1 large onion (finely chopped)
- 2 garlic cloves (crushed)
- 1 lb/450g minced lamb
- ½ cup/125 ml water
- 1 x 14 oz/400g can chopped tomatoes
- 2 tbsp tomato paste/puree
- 1 tsp ground cinnamon
- ½ tsp salt
- ½ tsp freshly ground black pepper
- 1 medium eggplant/aubergine (cut into 1 inch/2-3cm pieces)
- 5 oz/150g feta (crumbled)
- 1 large handful of fresh mint (chopped)
- Salad and warm toasted pitta to serve

PREPARATION STEPS

1. Press the sauté button on the Instant Pot on normal heat, (custom level 3 for the Evo Plus).
2. Once display says HOT, add 1 tbsp of the olive oil.
3. Add 1 large onion (finely chopped), and 2 garlic cloves (crushed), sauté until soft, stir regularly.
4. Add 1 lb/450g minced lamb, cook for 10 minutes until browned, stir occasionally.
5. Drain off the mince, add ½ cup/125 ml water, 1 x 14 oz/400g can chopped tomatoes, 2 tbsp tomato paste/puree, 1 tsp ground cinnamon, ½ tsp salt, and ½ tsp freshly ground black pepper. Press cancel.
6. Place the lid on the Instant Pot, set valve to seal, select manual high pressure (pressure cook custom high on Evo Plus) for 10 minutes.
7. When Instant Pot beeps, allow 5 minutes before releasing the pressure.
8. When pin drops, open the lid. Press cancel.
9. Press the sauté button on the Instant Pot on normal heat, (custom level 3 for the Evo Plus).
10. Stir in 1 medium eggplant/aubergine (cut into 1 inch/2-3cm pieces). Cook for a few minutes until soft.
11. Serve sprinkled with 5 oz/150g feta (crumbled), 1 large handful of fresh mint (chopped), salad, and warm toasted pitta.

Rotisserie Döner (Shawarma) Kebab

Using a special mix to capture that fantastic Shawarma flavour.

SERVES 4

INGREDIENTS

- 1 tsp all-purpose/plain flour
- 1 tsp dried oregano
- ½ tsp dried Italian herbs
- ½ tsp garlic powder
- ½ tsp onion powder
- ¼ tsp cayenne pepper
- 1 tsp salt
- ½ tsp freshly ground black pepper
- 1 lb/450g lamb mince
- Trivet
- 1 cup/250 ml water for steam
- Foil

PREPARATION STEPS

1. In a large bowl, combine 1 tsp all-purpose/plain flour, 1 tsp dried oregano, ½ tsp dried Italian herbs, ½ tsp garlic powder, ½ tsp onion powder, ¼ tsp cayenne pepper, 1 tsp salt, and ½ tsp freshly ground black pepper.

2. Add 1 lb/450g lamb mince and mix thoroughly, kneading by hand for 2 to 3 minutes, until it is extremely smooth, or mix in a food processor.

3. Turn meat out onto a clean work surface. Wet hands with water, then shape into an even block 20 cm/8 inch long.

4. Wrap tightly in kitchen foil, roll up into an even log shape, twist the ends and snip off excess foil.

5. Add 1 cup/250 ml of water to the pot, place the log on the trivet, and lower the trivet into the pot.

6. Place the lid on the Instant Pot, set valve to seal, select manual high pressure (pressure cook custom high on Evo Plus) for 30 minutes.

7. When Instant Pot beeps, allow 10 minutes before releasing the pressure. In the meantime, pre heat a foil lined baking tray with a rack on in your oven, to 450 °/f/230 °/c.

8. When pin drops on the Instant Pot, open the lid. Press cancel.

9. Remove the foil from the log and place it on a rack on the pre heated foil lined baking tray.

10. Bake for 10 to 15 minutes, rotating once until browned evenly.

11. Once cooked, remove from the oven, cover with foil, and allow to rest for 10 minutes. Reserve any juices from baking tray.

12. Slice meat very thinly, only carving as much as you intend to use.

13. Press the sauté button on the Instant Pot on normal heat, (custom level 3 for the Evo Plus).

14. Once display says HOT add the meat, cook until lightly coloured but still floppy, adding reserved juices if desired.

15. Serve with toasted Pitta bread, salad, jalapenos, and kebab sauces.

Liver & Onions

A traditional British dish, very tender when cooked in the Instant Pot.

SERVES 4

INGREDIENTS

- 1 lb/450g lambs' liver
- 1 oz/25g unsalted butter
- 1 tbsp vegetable oil
- 2 tbsp all-purpose/plain flour
- 1 onion (sliced)
- 4.5 oz/125g smoked bacon slices (each cut into 4-5 pieces)
- 1 cup beef stock
- 1-2 tsp tomato ketchup
- Salt and freshly ground black pepper (to taste)

PREPARATION STEPS

1. Rinse 1 lb/450g lambs liver under cold water in a colander, drain well, and place on paper towel.

2. Press the sauté button on the Instant Pot on normal heat, (custom level 3 for the Evo Plus).

3. Add half the 1 oz/25g of unsalted butter, and 1 tbsp vegetable oil to the pot.

4. In a bowl, place 1 tbsp of the 2 tbsp all-purpose/plain flour, season with plenty of salt and freshly ground black pepper.

5. Add half the liver to the bowl and toss lightly in the flour to coat. Place each piece carefully in the hot fat and cook 1-2 minutes on each side until lightly browned, but not completely cooked through. Transfer to a plate. Toss the remaining liver in the seasoned flour, brown in the pot as before. Transfer to the same plate as the first batch.

6. Melt the remaining butter in the pot, add 1 onion (sliced), cook 1 minute, stirring to separate the layers.

7. Add 4.5 oz/125g smoked bacon slices (each cut into 4-5 pieces), cook together for 8 to 10 minutes, or until the onion is pale golden brown and the bacon is beginning to crisp. Stir often.

8. Sprinkle the rest of the flour over the onion and bacon, stir it for a few seconds.

9. Stir in 1 cup of beef stock, and 1-2 tsp tomato ketchup to deglaze the pot. Press cancel.

10. Place reserved liver pieces back into the pot.

11. Place the lid on the Instant Pot, set valve to seal, select manual low pressure (pressure cook custom low on Evo Plus) for 5 minutes.

12. When Instant Pot beeps, allow 5 minutes before releasing the pressure.

13. When pin drops, open the lid.

14. Serve the liver and bacon with mashed potatoes, and freshly cooked greens.

Summer Lamb with Mint & Tomato

Mint and lamb, a match made in heaven, with a rich fresh tomato sauce.

SERVES 4

INGREDIENTS

- 1 lb/450g ripe tomatoes (peeled)
- 1 lb/450g cubed lamb (shoulder or leg)
- 2 tbsp olive oil
- Salt and freshly ground black pepper (to season the lamb)
- 1 medium onion (thinly sliced)
- 2 cloves garlic (crushed)
- 0.4 cup/100 ml lamb stock (from cubes or powdered)
- 1 tbsp tomato paste/puree
- ¼ tsp salt
- ¼ tsp freshly ground black pepper
- 5 oz/150g jarred artichoke hearts in oil (drained)
- 1 small handful of fresh mint leaves (roughly chopped)
- 1 tbsp cornstarch/cornflour
- 1 tbsp cold water

PREPARATION STEPS

1. Make a cross in the bottom of each of the 1 lb/450g tomatoes, put them in a large bowl and pour boiling water over them, leave them for one minute. Drain and peel.

2. Press the sauté button on the Instant Pot on normal heat, (custom level 3 for the Evo Plus).

3. Season 1 lb/450g cubed lamb (shoulder or leg) with salt and freshly ground black pepper.

4. Once display says HOT, add 1 tbsp of the olive oil.

5. Sauté the lamb until browned, remove from the pot.

6. Add the remaining oil, sauté 1 medium onion (thinly sliced), and 2 cloves garlic (crushed) for about 3 minutes until soft.

7. Return the lamb to the pot, stir in the tomatoes, 0.4 cup/100 ml lamb stock (from cubes or powdered), 1 tbsp tomato paste/puree, ¼ tsp salt, and ¼ tsp freshly ground black pepper. Bring to the boil, then press cancel.

8. Place the lid on the Instant Pot, set valve to seal, select manual high pressure (pressure cook custom high on Evo Plus) for 20 minutes.

9. When Instant Pot beeps, allow 10 minutes before releasing the pressure.

10. When pin drops, open the lid.

11. Mix 1 tbsp cornstarch/cornflour with 1 tbsp cold water, add to the pot, stir to thicken.

12. Stir in 5 oz/150g of jarred artichoke hearts in oil (drained,) and 1 small handful of fresh mint leaves (roughly chopped). Serve with rice, or potatoes.

Lamb Rogan Josh

A blissful fall apart lamb curry.

SERVES 4

INGREDIENTS

- 3 ½ tbsp ghee
- 1 small cinnamon stick
- 6 green cardamom pods
- 4 cloves
- 1 large onion (finely chopped)
- 1 handful fresh cilantro/coriander (stalks, leaves reserved)
- 3 garlic cloves (finely chopped)
- 1 tbsp fresh ginger (finely grated)
- 2 tbsp paprika
- ¾ tsp Kashmiri chilli powder
- 1 heaped tbsp ground cilantro/coriander
- 1 heaped tbsp ground cumin
- 2 tsp turmeric powder
- ¼ tsp nutmeg
- 1 tsp garam masala
- ½ tsp fennel powder
- 5 tbsp tomato puree/sauce/passata
- 1 tsp salt
- 1 cup/250ml chicken stock
- 1.5 lb/700g boneless lamb shoulder (1.2 inch/3 cm cubes)
- ½ cup/125 ml plain yogurt
- Handful reserved fresh cilantro/coriander leaves

PREPARATION STEPS

1. Press the sauté button on the Instant Pot on normal heat, (custom level 3 for the Evo Plus).
2. Once display says HOT, add 3 ½ tbsp ghee, 1 small cinnamon stick, 6 green cardamom pods, and 4 cloves. Cook for 1 minute stirring regularly.
3. Add 1 large onion (finely chopped), cook for 7 minutes stirring frequently, until it starts to brown at the edges.
4. Add 1 handful fresh cilantro/coriander stalks, (leaves reserved), 3 garlic cloves (finely chopped), and 1 tbsp fresh ginger (finely grated). Cook for 1 minute stirring regularly.
5. Stir in 2 tbsp paprika, ¾ tsp Kashmiri chilli powder, 1 heaped tbsp ground cilantro/coriander, 1 heaped tbsp ground cumin, 2 tsp turmeric powder, ¼ tsp nutmeg, 1 tsp garam masala, and ½ tsp fennel powder. Cook for 20 seconds stirring continuously.
6. Stir in 5 tbsp tomato puree/sauce/passata, 1 tsp salt, and 1 cup/250 ml chicken stock, Add 1.5 lb/700g boneless lamb shoulder (1.2 inch/3 cm cubes).
7. Stir well, then press cancel.
8. Place lid on Instant Pot, set valve to seal, select manual high pressure (pressure cook custom high on Evo Plus) for 20 minutes.
9. When Instant Pot beeps, allow 10 minutes before releasing the pressure.
10. Stir in ½ cup/125 ml plain yogurt, and extra garam masala to taste.
11. Garnish with a handful of reserved fresh cilantro/coriander leaves.

PREPARATION STEPS

1. Press the sauté button on the Instant Pot on normal heat, (custom level 3 for the Evo Plus).

2. Once display says HOT, add 3 tbsp vegetable oil, 1 tsp garlic (finely chopped), 1 tsp fresh ginger (finely chopped), 3 bay leaves, 6 cardamon pods, 3 inch/5cm cinnamon sticks and 1 medium tomato (diced). Stir for 30 seconds.

3. Add 2 medium onions (diced) and 1 ½ tsp salt, stir, then place a lid or plate on the pot (the Instant Pot glass lid, or any lid that fits), allow to sweat for 5 minutes, stir occasionally.

4. Add 1 lb/450g minced lamb, beef, or chicken, cook until browned, stir occasionally.

5. Stir in ½ tsp turmeric powder, ½ tsp cumin powder, 1 tsp curry powder, 1 tsp cilantro/coriander powder, and 1 tsp Kashmiri chilli powder.

6. Cook for 5 minutes with the glass lid on, stir occasionally.

7. Add 2 medium potatoes (peeled and diced 1 inch/2.5 cm), and 1 cup/250 ml of hot water. Press cancel.

8. Place the lid on the Instant Pot, set valve to seal, select manual high pressure (pressure cook custom high on Evo Plus) for 10 minutes.

9. When Instant Pot beeps, allow 10 minutes before releasing the pressure.

10. When pin drops, open the lid.

11. Stir in ½ tsp garam masala, 2 birds eye chillies (halved lengthways), and 1 handful of fresh cilantro/coriander.

12. Serve with rice or naan.

Keema Aloo

Authentic Bengali minced meat curry.

SERVES 4

INGREDIENTS

- 3 tbsp vegetable oil
- 1 tsp garlic (finely chopped)
- 1 tsp fresh ginger (finely chopped)
- 3 bay leaves
- 6 cardamon pods
- 3 x 2 inch/5cm cinnamon sticks
- 1 medium tomato (diced)
- 2 medium onions (diced)
- 1 ½ tsp salt
- 1 lb/450g minced lamb, beef, or chicken
- ½ tsp turmeric powder
- ½ tsp cumin powder
- 1 tsp curry powder
- 1 tsp cilantro/coriander powder
- 1 tsp Kashmiri chilli powder
- 2 medium potatoes (peeled and diced 1 inch/2.5 cm)
- 1 cup/250 ml hot water
- ½ tsp garam masala
- 2 birds eye chillies (halved lengthways)
- 1 handful fresh cilantro/coriander

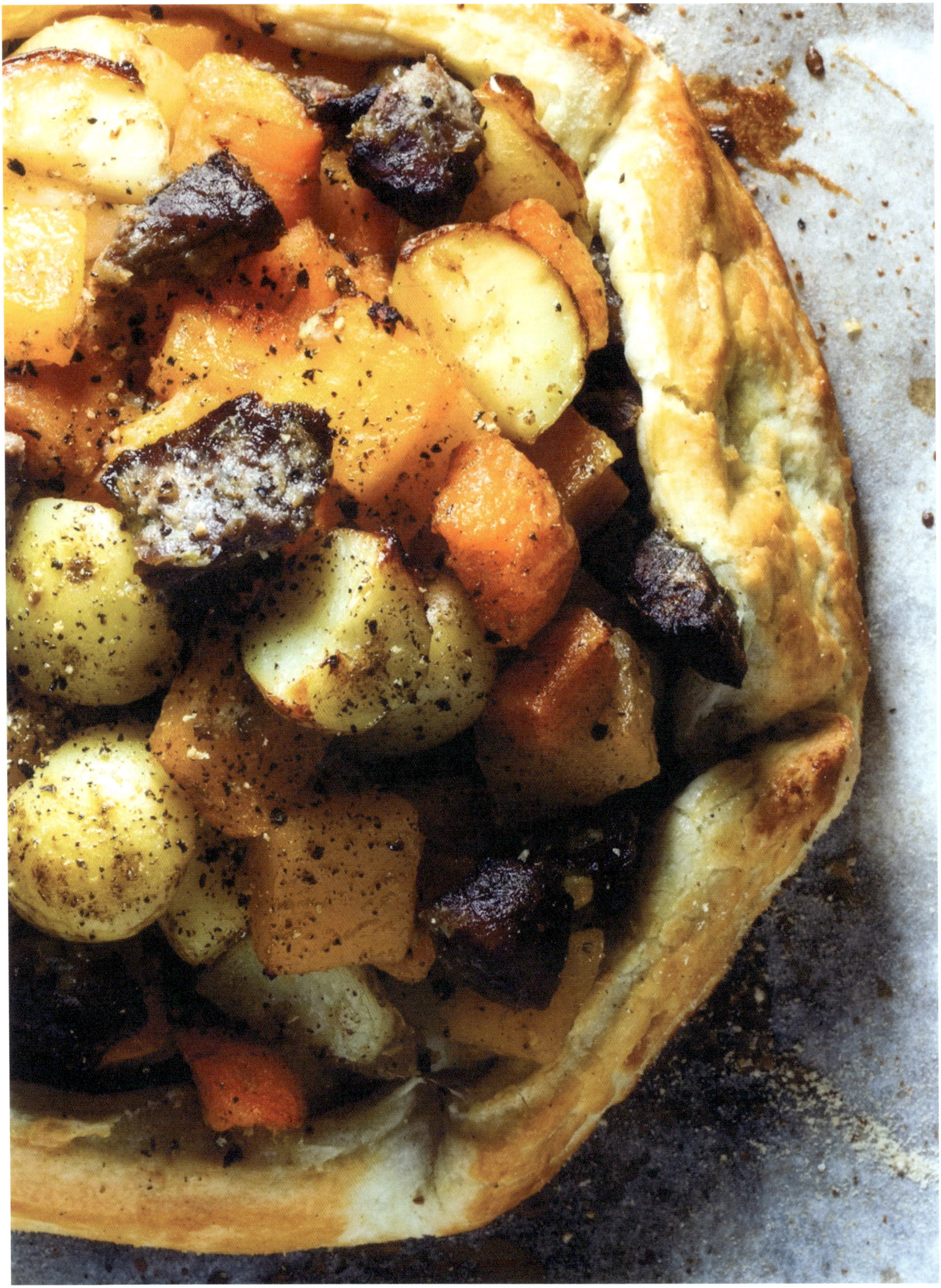

Beef

Texas Red

Thick and hearty Chili, also known as Texas Red.

Pressure cooked in a fraction of the traditional cooking time.

SERVES 4

INGREDIENTS

- 1 tbsp olive oil
- 2 lb/1 kg course minced beef
- 1 tbsp onion granules
- 2 cups/500 ml passata/tomato sauce
- 4 tsp Kashmiri chili powder
- 1 tsp garlic powder
- 1 tsp cumin powder
- 1 tsp paprika
- ½ tsp cayenne pepper
- ½ tsp freshly ground black pepper
- 1 tsp chicken granules or 1 stock cube
- 1 tsp beef granules or 1 stock cube
- ½ tsp salt
- ¼ cup/60g tomato ketchup
- 1 cup/250 ml water

PREPARATION STEPS

1. Press the sauté button on the Instant Pot on normal heat, (custom level 3 for the Evo Plus) once display says HOT, heat 1 tbsp olive oil.
2. Add 2 lb/1 kg of course minced beef, lightly brown.
3. Drain off excess liquid.
4. Stir in 1 tbsp onion granules, sauté for a couple of minutes, stir regularly.
5. Add 2 cups/500 ml of passata/tomato sauce, cook for 5 minutes, stir regularly.
6. Add 4 tsp Kashmiri chili powder, 1 tsp garlic powder, 1 tsp cumin powder, 1 tsp paprika, ½ tsp cayenne pepper, ½ tsp freshly ground black pepper, 1 tsp chicken granules or 1 stock cube, 1 tsp beef granules or 1 stock cube, ½ tsp salt, ¼ cup/60g tomato ketchup, and 1 cup/250 ml of water. Press cancel.
7. Place lid on Instant Pot, set valve to seal, select manual high pressure (pressure cook custom high on Evo Plus) for 20 minutes.
8. When Instant Pot beeps, allow 10 minutes natural pressure release, then open the valve to release the rest of the pressure.
9. When pin drops, open the lid.
10. Check for seasoning.
11. Best served with grated cheese and sour cream.

INGREDIENTS

- 1 tbsp olive oil
- 1 lb/450g lean minced beef
- 1 beef stock cube
- ¾ tsp salt
- ½ tsp freshly ground black pepper
- 2 medium onions (roughly chopped)
- 10 oz/300g carrots (peeled, thickly sliced)
- 1 lb 4 oz/600g potatoes (peeled and cut into chunks)
- ¾ cup/180ml of hot water
- 1 x 14 oz/400g baked beans
- Worcestershire sauce to taste
- A handful of fresh parsley (roughly chopped)

PREPARATION STEPS

1. Press the sauté button on the Instant Pot on normal heat, (custom level 3 for the Evo Plus).

2. Once display says HOT, add 1 tbsp olive oil, and 1 lb/450g lean minced beef. Sauté until browned, stir regularly.

3. Crumble in 1 beef stock cube, ¾ tsp salt, and ½ tsp freshly ground black pepper, mix well.

4. Add 2 medium onions (roughly chopped), 10 oz/300g carrots (peeled, thickly sliced), 1 lb 4 oz/600g potatoes (peeled and cut into chunks), and ¾ cup/180ml of hot water. Press cancel.

5. Place the lid on the Instant Pot, set valve to seal, select manual high pressure (pressure cook custom high on Evo Plus) for 15 minutes.

6. When Instant Pot beeps, allow 5 minutes before releasing the pressure.

7. When pin drops, open the lid.

8. Stir in 1 x 14 oz/400g baked beans, and Worcestershire sauce to taste. Press cancel.

9. Press sauté as above, heat for a couple of minutes. Press cancel.

10. Check seasoning, serve sprinkled with a handful of fresh parsley (roughly chopped).

Beef & Beans

A tasty and quick midweek meal.

SERVES 4

Beef Stroganoff

A beautiful classic Russian dish.

SERVES 6

INGREDIENTS

- 2 lb/900g beef short rib (bone in ½ inch/2 cm thick)
- 2 tsp vegetable oil
- Salt and freshly ground black pepper
- 2 tbsp olive oil
- 1 tsp salted butter
- 1 medium onion (sliced)
- 3 garlic cloves (crushed)
- 8 oz/230g chestnut mushrooms (thickly sliced)
- 3 tbsp Dijon mustard
- 1 cup/250 ml beef stock
- ½ cup/125 ml crème fraiche

PREPARATION STEPS

1. For best results, use a heavy gauge cast iron pan.
2. Heat the cast iron pan on full heat.
3. Meanwhile coat the 2 lb/900g beef short rib (bone in ½ inch/2 cm thick), with 2 tsp vegetable oil, season with salt and freshly ground black pepper.
4. Once the pan starts to smoke, sear the beef for 40 seconds on each side.
5. Remove beef, allow to rest.
6. If you wish to use your Instant Pot instead of a pan, it will still do a good job, however not quite as good as a cast iron pan.
7. If you wish to sear your steak in your Instant Pot, press the sauté button on the Instant Pot on high heat, (custom level 6 for the Evo Plus). Once the display says HOT, sear the beef for 40 to 60 seconds on each side.
8. Remove beef and allow to rest.
9. Add to the pot, 2 tbsp olive oil, 1 tsp salted butter, 1 medium onion (sliced) and 3 garlic cloves (crushed). Sauté for a couple of minutes stirring regularly. Add 8 oz/230g chestnut mushrooms (thickly sliced), sauté for further 2 minutes, stirring regularly.
10. Stir in 3 tbsp Dijon mustard, and 1 cup/250 ml beef stock, scraping anything from the bottom of the pot with a wooden spatula. Press cancel.
11. Add the beef to the Instant Pot covering with the lid. Set valve to seal, select manual high pressure (pressure cook custom high on Evo Plus) for 30 minutes.
12. When Instant Pot beeps, allow 10 minutes before releasing the pressure.
13. When pin drops, open the lid. Press cancel.
14. Stir in ½ cup/125 ml crème fraiche, and season to taste.
15. Serve with mashed potatoes and fresh vegetables.

Seared Steak Stew

Seared and rested before slicing - adds so much to the flavour.

SERVES 4

INGREDIENTS

- 1 lb/450g braising steak
- 2 tsp vegetable oil
- Salt and freshly ground black pepper
- 2 tbsp olive oil
- 1 tsp salted butter
- 1 medium onion (sliced)
- 3 garlic cloves (crushed)
- 4 medium carrots (chopped 1 inch/2.5 cm)
- 2 celery sticks (chopped 1 inch/2.5 cm)
- ¼ tsp baking soda/sodium bicarbonate (not baking powder)
- 1 ¾ cups/400 ml beef stock
- 1 handful dried pearl barley
- ¼ tsp salt
- 8 oz/230g chestnut mushrooms (sliced in half)
- 2 medium tomatoes (quartered)
- 2 tbsp cornstarch/cornflour
- 2 tbsp cold water

PREPARATION STEPS

1. For best results, use a heavy gauge cast iron pan.
2. Heat the cast iron pan on full heat.
3. Meanwhile coat the 1 lb/450g braising steak with 2 tsp vegetable oil, season with salt and freshly ground black pepper.
4. Once the pan starts to smoke, sear the steak for 40 seconds on each side.
5. Remove steak, allow to rest.
6. If you wish to use your Instant Pot instead of a pan it will still do a good job, however not quite as good as a cast iron pan.
7. If you wish to sear your steak in your Instant Pot, press the sauté button on the Instant Pot on high heat, (custom level 6 for the Evo Plus). Once the display says HOT, sear the steak for 40 to 60 seconds on each side. Press cancel.
8. Remove steak and allow to rest.
9. Press the sauté button on the Instant Pot on normal heat, (custom level 3 for the Evo Plus).
10. Once display says HOT, add 2 tbsp of olive oil, 1 tsp salted butter, 1 medium onion (sliced), 3 garlic cloves (crushed), 4 medium carrots (chopped 1 inch/2.5 cm), 2 celery sticks (chopped 1 inch/2.5 cm), and ¼ tsp baking soda/sodium bicarbonate (not baking powder).
11. Sauté, stirring regularly for about 5 minutes. Press cancel.
12. Add 1 ¾ cups/400 ml beef stock, 1 handful dried pearl barley and ¼ tsp salt.
13. Cut reserved steak into approx 1 inch/3 cm pieces, add to the pot. Finally add 8 oz/230g chestnut mushrooms (sliced in half), and 2 medium tomatoes (quartered).
14. Place the lid on the Instant Pot, set valve to seal, select manual high pressure (pressure cook custom high on Evo Plus) for 20 minutes.
15. When Instant Pot beeps, allow 10 minutes before releasing the pressure.
16. When pin drops, open the lid. Press cancel.
17. Press the sauté button on the Instant Pot on normal heat, (custom level 3 for the Evo Plus).
18. Mix 2 tbsp cornstarch/cornflour with 2 tbsp cold water
19. Slowly stir in all of the slurry, or until desired consistency is reached, being careful not to break up the vegetables.
20. Perfect served with mashed potatoes, or instead add a few new potatoes at step 10.

Goulash

A classic Hungarian stew.

SERVES 4

INGREDIENTS

- 1 lb/450g braising steak
- 2 tsp vegetable oil
- Salt and freshly ground black pepper
- 1 tbsp olive oil
- 1 tsp unsalted butter
- 1 medium onion (sliced)
- 3 garlic cloves (crushed)
- 8 oz/230g chestnut mushrooms (sliced in half)
- 1 tbsp paprika
- 1 lb/450g baby new potatoes (washed and halved)
- 0.4 cup/100 ml passata/tomato sauce/strained tomatoes
- 1.3 cup/300 ml beef stock
- 1 tsp dried thyme
- 2 tbsp cornstarch/cornflour
- 2 tbsp cold water
- ½ cup/125g natural yogurt
- Handful roughly chopped parsley leaves to serve and garnish.

PREPARATION STEPS

1. For best results, use a heavy gauge cast iron pan.
2. Heat the cast iron pan on full heat.
3. Meanwhile coat the 1 lb/450g braising steak with 2 tsp vegetable oil and season with salt and freshly ground black pepper.
4. Once the pan starts to smoke, sear the steak for 40 seconds on each side.
5. Remove steak and allow to rest.
6. If you wish to use your Instant Pot instead of a pan it will still do a good job, however not quite as good as a cast iron pan.
7. If you wish to sear your steak in your Instant, press the sauté button on the Instant Pot on high heat, (custom level 6 for the Evo Plus). Once the display says HOT, sear the steak for 40 to 60 seconds on each side. Press cancel.
8. Remove steak and allow to rest.
9. Press the sauté button on the Instant Pot on normal heat, (custom level 3 for the Evo Plus).
10. Once display says HOT, add 1 tbsp of olive oil, 1 tsp unsalted butter, 1 medium onion (sliced), 3 garlic cloves (crushed), 8 oz/230g chestnut mushrooms (sliced in half), and ½ tsp salt.
11. Sauté for 3 minutes until golden, stir regularly.
12. Cut reserved steak into approx 1 inch/3 cm pieces, add to the pot with 1 tbsp paprika, stir briefly, then add 1 lb/450g baby new potatoes (washed and halved), 0.4 cup/100 ml passata/tomato sauce/strained tomatoes, 1.3 cup/300 ml beef stock, and 1 tsp dried thyme. Stir, and press cancel.
13. Place the lid on the Instant Pot, set valve to seal, select manual high pressure (pressure cook custom high on Evo Plus) for 20 minutes.
14. When Instant Pot beeps, allow 10 minutes before releasing the pressure.
15. When pin drops, open the lid. Press cancel.
16. Press the sauté button on the Instant Pot on normal heat, (custom level 3 for the Evo Plus).
17. Mix 2 tbsp cornstarch/cornflour with 2 tbsp cold water, add to the pot, stir to thicken. Press cancel.
18. Taste for seasoning, serve topped with ½ cup/125g natural yogurt, and a handful of roughly chopped parsley leaves.

Beef Bourguignon

A traditional French stew made with beef braised in red wine.

SERVES 4

INGREDIENTS

- 1 lb/450g braising steak
- 1 ½ cups/375 ml red wine
- 3 garlic cloves (crushed)
- 1 bouquet garni
- 2 tsp vegetable oil
- 2 tbsp olive oil
- 7 oz/200g smoked bacon (cut into 1 inch/2.5 cm pieces)
- 1 onion (chopped)
- 1 carrot (chopped ¾ inch/2 cm)
- 7 oz/200g whole button mushrooms
- 7 oz/200g shallots (whole peeled)
- 2 tbsp cornstarch/cornflour
- 2 tbsp cold water
- Salt and freshly ground black pepper to taste

PREPARATION STEPS

1. Add 1 lb/450g braising steak, 1 ½ cups/375 ml red wine, 3 garlic cloves (crushed) and 1 bouquet garni to a bowl. Cover, and place in the fridge for at least 3 hours or preferably overnight.
2. Using a strainer, drain the meat, keep the left over marinade, and the bouquet garni, pat dry the meat using kitchen towel.
3. For the next stage use a heavy gauge cast iron pan for best results. (see step 9 to sear using Instant Pot).
4. Heat the cast iron pan on full heat.
5. Meanwhile coat the braising steak with 2 tsp vegetable oil, season with salt and freshly ground black pepper.
6. Once the pan starts to smoke, sear the steak for 40 seconds on each side.
7. Remove steak and allow to rest.
8. If you wish to use your Instant Pot instead of a pan, it will still do a good job, however not quite as good as a cast iron pan.
9. To sear your steak in your Instant Pot, press the sauté button on the Instant Pot on high heat, (custom level 6 for the Evo Plus). Once the display says HOT, sear the steak for 40 to 60 seconds on each side. Press cancel.
10. Remove steak and allow to rest.
11. Press the sauté button on the Instant Pot on normal heat, (custom level 3 for the Evo Plus).
12. Add 2 tbsp of olive oil, and 7 oz/200g smoked bacon (cut into 1 inch/2.5 cm pieces), sauté until crisp, stir regularly.
13. Add 1 onion (chopped), 1 carrot (chopped), and 7 oz/200g button mushrooms, sauté for a further 5 minutes stirring regularly. Deglaze with a little of the red wine marinade if the bottom of the pot starts to burn.
14. Pour the reserved marinade into the pot to deglaze anything that may have caught on the bottom of the pot.
15. Cut the reserved meat into 1 inch/3 cm cubes, stir into the pot. Place 7oz/200g shallots (whole peeled) on the top (to avoid overcooking).
16. Place the lid on the Instant Pot, set valve to seal, select manual high pressure (pressure cook custom high on Evo Plus) for 20 minutes.
17. When Instant Pot beeps, allow 10 minutes before releasing the pressure.
18. When pin drops, open the lid. Press cancel.
19. Add salt and freshly ground black pepper to taste.
20. Mix 2 tbsp cornstarch/cornflour with 2 tbsp cold water.
21. Press sauté as above, slowly stir in the cornstarch/cornflour slurry a little at a time, until desired consistency is reached, being careful not to break up the vegetables. Press cancel.
22. Enjoy with mashed potatoes and French beans.

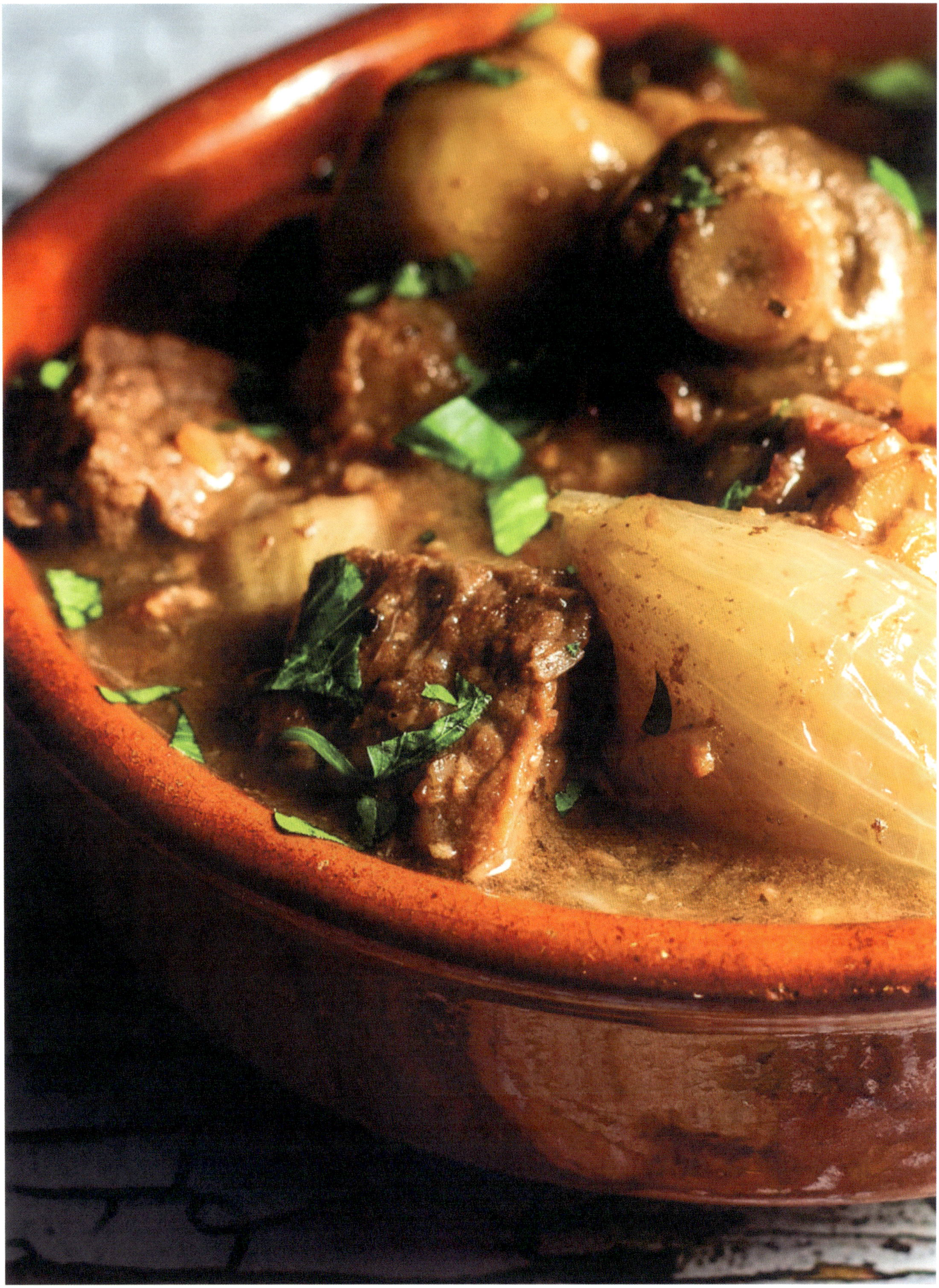

PREPARATION STEPS

1. Add 1 cup/250 ml beef stock, ½ lb/225g braising steak (¾ inch/2 cm pieces), 1 cup new potatoes (¾ inch/2 cm pieces), 1 cup carrots (¾ inch/2 cm pieces), 1 cup swede (¾ inch/2 cm pieces), 1 medium onion (sliced), ½ tsp salt, and ½ tsp freshly ground black pepper to the pot.
2. Place the lid on the Instant Pot, set valve to seal, select manual high pressure (pressure cook custom high on Evo Plus) for 15 minutes.
3. When Instant Pot beeps, press cancel.
4. Allow 10 minutes before releasing the pressure.
5. When pin drops, open the lid.
6. Using a slotted spoon, carefully add meat and vegetables to a colander over a bowl. Once cool, and liquid has drained, reserve meat and vegetables, add the liquid back to the pot, gently stir in ¼ tsp of white pepper.
7. Place 1 lb/450g of pre-made short crust pastry onto a piece of baking parchment, lightly flour the surface of the parchment and the dough.
8. Roll out the dough and trim into a 10 inch/25 cm round circle, ¼ of an inch/0.6 cm thick. Place the filling in the middle of the circle. Fold up the sides of the dough 2 inches/5 cm and press onto the filling to secure.
9. Lift the parchment paper and galette, and place onto the baking sheet.
10. In a small bowl, whisk the egg yolk, and 1 tbsp milk. Brush the galette pastry with the wash, spray a little oil onto the filling, and place the baking sheet into the oven.
11. Bake in a pre-heated oven at 350 °/f/180 °/c for 20 minutes, or until the crust has turned golden brown.
12. Press the sauté button on the Instant Pot on normal heat, (custom level 3 for the Evo Plus).
13. Mix in 1 tbsp cornstarch/cornflour with 1 tbsp cold water.
14. Add the previously drained liquid to the Instant Pot, once the liquid in the pot starts to bubble slowly, add the cornstarch slurry, until required consistency is reached.
15. Season to taste and pour over the Galette generously.
16. Serve with fresh greens.

Cornish Galette

All the character of a Cornish Pasty combined with the ease of a French Galette.

SERVES 4

INGREDIENTS

- 1 cup/250 ml beef stock
- ½ lb/225g braising steak (¾ inch/2 cm pieces)
- 1 cup new potatoes (¾ inch/2 cm pieces)
- 1 cup carrots (¾ inch/2 cm pieces)
- 1 cup swede (¾ inch/2 cm pieces)
- 1 medium onion (sliced)
- ½ tsp salt
- ½ tsp freshly ground black pepper
- ¼ tsp ground white pepper
- 1 lb/450g pre-made short crust pastry
- All-purpose/plain flour (for dusting)
- 1 tbsp cornstarch/cornflour
- 1 tbsp cold water

Sous Vide Steak & Vegetables

A great way of getting to grips with cooking sous vide.

SERVES 2

INGREDIENTS

- 1 lb/450g baby potatoes
- 6 baby carrots
- 10 asparagus spears
- 4 shallots
- 1 oz/30g unsalted butter
- Salt and freshly ground black pepper to taste
- 2 x 12 oz/340g striploin/sirloin steaks
- 6 garlic cloves (crushed)
- 2 sprigs of rosemary
- 6 sprigs of thyme

PREPARATION STEPS

1. Fill inner pot to just under maximum level with hot water.
2. Select sous vide mode, custom 190 °/f/87 °/c, bring up to temperature.
3. Have 3 sous vide compatible zipper type bags ready to fill.
4. Add 1 lb/450g baby potatoes, 6 baby carrots, 4 shallots, 0.7 oz/20g of the unsalted butter, salt and freshly ground black pepper to the first bag.
5. Remove as much of the air as you can by lowering the bag into a bowl of water, using the water to push the air out of the bag, being careful not to allow any water into the bag. Seal while immersed or use a vacuum sealer.
6. When the Instant Pot has come to temperature, place the bag of vegetables in the pot, close the lid making sure the valve is open, cook for 1 hour.
7. In the meantime, season 2 x 12 oz/340g striploin/sirloin steaks well on both sides with salt and freshly ground black pepper.
8. Transfer steaks to the second bag, arrange them side by side, along with 6 garlic cloves (crushed), 2 sprigs of rosemary, and 6 sprigs of thyme. Set to one side.
9. In the third bag, 10 asparagus spears, 0.35 oz/10g unsalted butter, add salt and freshly ground black pepper to taste.
10. As before, remove as much of the air from the bags as you can. Seal and set to one side at room temperature.
11. After the vegetables have been in the water bath for 1 hour, reduce the temperature to 130 °/f/54 °/c by replacing some of the hot water with cold. Check with a thermometer.
12. Add the steaks, asparagus, and with the vegetables still in the pot, cook for another hour.
13. Remove the steaks from the bag, pat dry with kitchen towel.
14. In heat safe place on a wire rack, using a kitchen blowtorch to sear the steaks until golden brown, or apply a little high smoke point cooking oil to them, then sear quickly (to avoid cooking through) on both sides and edges, in a very hot preheated, preferably heavy gauge pan.
15. Serve alongside the buttered sous vide vegetables.

- 1 tbsp soy sauce
- 2 tbsp tomato paste/puree
- ½ cup/80g dry sundried tomatoes
- 1 tsp Italian herbs
- 1 tsp vegetable bouillon
- ½ cup/125 ml red wine
- 1 ¾ cups/420 ml cold water
- 5 ½ oz/150g spaghetti (snapped in half)
- Grated parmesan to serve

PREPARATION STEPS

1. Heat oven to 400 °/f/200 °/c.
2. Spread 1 lb/450g of minced beef evenly onto a shallow tray, season with ¼ tsp salt and ¼ tsp freshly ground black pepper.
3. Roast for about 15 minutes, turning halfway through until nicely browned.
4. In the meantime, add to the cold pot, 1 tbsp olive oil, and 4 slices of smoked bacon (½ inch/1 cm dice).
5. Press the sauté button on the Instant Pot on normal heat, (custom level 3 for the Evo Plus).
6. Cook the bacon until crisp (cooking bacon from cold helps to render the fat more efficiently from the meat which results in crispier bacon).
7. Add 1 large onion (chopped), 2 medium carrots (peeled and chopped ½ inch/1cm and ¼ tsp baking soda/sodium bicarbonate (not baking powder). Baking soda speeds things up a little.
8. Cook for a few minutes until vegetables start to soften.
9. Add roasted beef, 1 ½ cups/200g sliced mushrooms, 1 x 14 oz/400g can of chopped tomatoes, 1 tbsp soy sauce, 2 tbsp tomato paste/puree, ½ cup/80g dry sundried tomatoes, 1 tsp Italian herbs, 1 tsp vegetable bouillon, and ½ cup/125 ml red wine.
10. Deglaze the pan for a minute or two, before adding 1 ¾ cups/420 ml of cold water, stir and add 5 ½ oz/150g spaghetti (snapped in half), making sure it is covered by the liquid.
11. Place lid on Instant Pot, set valve to seal, select manual high pressure (pressure cook custom high on Evo Plus) for 7 minutes.
12. When Instant Pot beeps, allow 10 minutes natural pressure release, open the valve to release the rest of the pressure.
13. When pin drops, open the lid.
14. Check for seasoning.
15. Grate parmesan to serve.

Roasted Beef Spaghetti Bolognese

Take your Bolognaise up a level with sundried tomatoes, red wine, and roasted minced beef.

SERVES 4

INGREDIENTS

- 1 lb/450g ground/minced beef
- ¼ tsp salt
- ¼ tsp freshly ground black pepper
- 1 tbsp olive oil
- 4 slices of smoked bacon (½ inch/1 cm dice)
- 1 large onion (chopped)
- 3 garlic cloves (crushed)
- 2 medium carrots (peeled and chopped ½ inch/1cm)
- ¼ tsp baking soda/sodium bicarbonate (not baking powder)
- 1 ½ cups/200g sliced mushrooms
- 1 x 14 oz/400g can chopped tomatoes

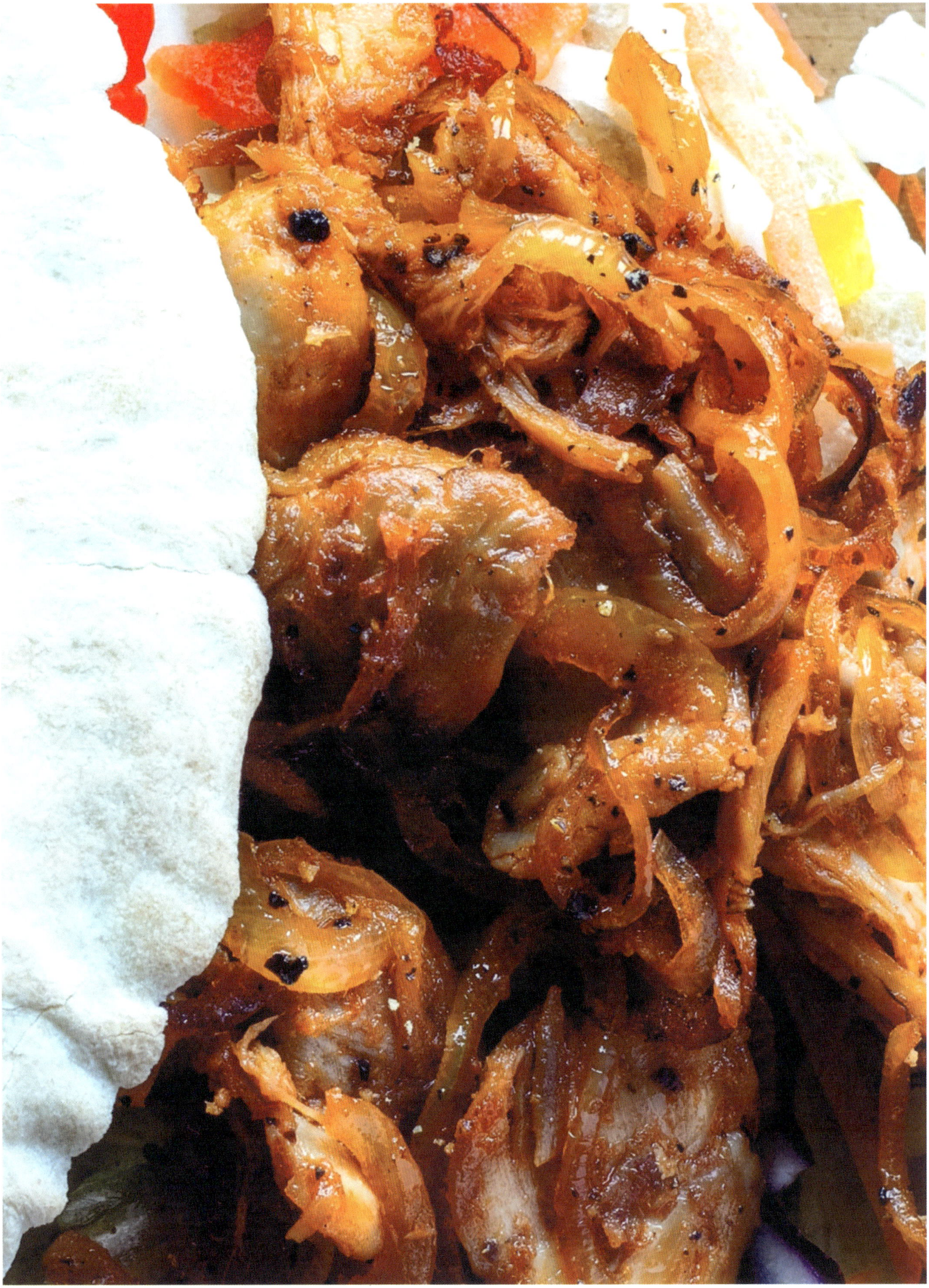

Chicken

Moroccan Lemon Chicken

A rich and fragrant Moroccan chicken stew.

SERVES 4

INGREDIENTS

- 1 ½ tsp ground cumin
- ½ tsp ground cilantro/coriander
- ½ tsp onion powder
- ½ tsp garlic powder
- ½ tsp paprika
- ¼ tsp freshly ground black pepper
- ½ tsp salt
- 8 chicken thighs (de-boned & skinless)
- 2 tbsp olive oil
- 1 medium onion (sliced)
- 3 garlic cloves (crushed)
- 1 whole preserved lemon (finely chopped)
- ¾ cup/100g whole blanched almonds
- ¾ cup/140g green olives (pitted)
- ¾ cup/180 ml chicken stock
- Large handful chopped cilantro/coriander
- Salt and freshly ground black pepper (to taste)
- 1 tbsp cornstarch/cornflour
- 1 tbsp cold water

PREPARATION STEPS

1. In a bowl, combine 1 ½ tsp ground cumin, ½ tsp ground cilantro/coriander, ½ tsp onion powder, ½ tsp garlic powder, ½ tsp paprika, ¼ tsp freshly ground black pepper, and ½ tsp salt.

2. Coat the 8 chicken thighs (de-boned & skinless) with the spices and set aside.

3. Press the sauté button on the Instant Pot on normal heat, (custom level 3 for the Evo Plus).

4. Once display says HOT, add 2 tbsp of olive oil.

5. Add 1 medium onion (sliced), and 3 garlic cloves (crushed), sauté for 2 minutes stirring regularly.

6. Add the coated chicken, sauté for another 2 minutes, stirring regularly. Press cancel.

7. Add 1 whole preserved lemon (finely chopped), ¾ cup/100g whole blanched almonds, ¾ cup/140g green olives (pitted), and ¾ cup/180 ml chicken stock.

8. Place the lid on the Instant Pot, set valve to seal, select manual high pressure (pressure cook custom high on Evo Plus) for 10 minutes.

9. When Instant Pot beeps, allow 10 minutes before releasing the pressure.

10. When pin drops, open the lid. Press cancel.

11. Press sauté as above, mix 1 tbsp cornstarch/cornflour with 1 tbsp cold water, stir in to thicken. Press cancel.

12. Stir in a large handful of chopped cilantro/coriander.

13. Season with salt and freshly ground black pepper.

14. Serve with vegetables, and rice or potatoes.

INGREDIENTS

- 2 tbsp vegetable oil
- 2 medium onions (finely chopped)
- 2 garlic cloves (finely chopped)
- ½ inch/1cm fresh ginger (grated)
- 1 green birds eye chilli (finely sliced)
- 1 tsp salt
- 2 tsp garam masala
- ½ tsp Kashmiri chilli powder
- 1 tbsp curry powder
- 2 lb/900g chicken breasts (cut into bite sized pieces)
- 1 ½ cups/375g passata/tomato sauce/strained tomatoes
- 1 tbsp tomato paste/puree
- ¼ cup/50g tomato ketchup
- ½ cup/125 ml coconut cream
- Fresh cilantro/coriander to garnish

PREPARATION STEPS

1. Press the sauté button on the Instant Pot on normal heat, (custom level 3 for the Evo Plus)
2. Once display says HOT, add 2 tbsp vegetable oil, 2 medium onions (finely chopped), 2 garlic cloves (finely chopped), ½ inch/1cm fresh ginger (grated), 1 green birds eye chilli (finely sliced), and 1 tsp salt.
3. Sauté for about 5 minutes, stirring regularly, until the onions are translucent.
4. Add 2 tsp garam masala, ½ tsp Kashmiri chilli powder, 1 tbsp curry powder, and 2 lb/900g chicken breasts, (cut into bite sized pieces) sauté for 1 minute, stir regularly.
5. Stir in 1 ½ cups/375g passata/tomato sauce/strained tomatoes, 1 tbsp tomato paste/puree, and ¼ cup/50g tomato ketchup.
6. Place the lid on the Instant Pot, set valve to seal, select manual low pressure (pressure cook custom low on Evo Plus) for 5 minutes.
7. When Instant Pot beeps, allow 5 minutes before releasing the pressure.
8. When pin drops, open the lid.
9. Stir in ½ cup/125 ml coconut cream.
10. Garnish with fresh cilantro/coriander.
11. Serve with rice and/or fresh warm naan.

Chicken Tikka Masala

Probably the most popular curry in the world.

SERVES 4

Chicken & Spring Vegetable Stew

A fresh and delicious dish-good enough to eat every day.

SERVES 4

INGREDIENTS

- 2.2lb/1kg chicken thighs (bone in, skin on)
- Salt and freshly ground black pepper to taste
- 2 tbsp unsalted butter
- 1 medium onion (sliced)
- 2 cloves of garlic (crushed)
- 1 lb/450g baby new potatoes (washed and halved)
- 1 ¾ cups/400 ml chicken or vegetable stock
- 1 tsp Dijon mustard
- 16 oz/400g mixed spring vegetables (broccoli florets, peas, broad beans, and sliced courgette)
- 4 tbsp crème fraiche
- Handful of fresh tarragon leaves (roughly chopped), or ½ tsp of dried tarragon
- 2 tbsp cornstarch/cornflour
- 2 tbsp cold water

PREPARATION STEPS

1. Press the sauté button on the Instant Pot on normal heat, (custom level 3 for the Evo Plus).
2. Season 8 chicken thighs (bone in, skin on) with salt and freshly ground black pepper to taste.
3. Once display says HOT, add 2 tbsp of unsalted butter.
4. Add the chicken thighs, sauté for about 5 minutes on each side until golden. Press cancel.
5. Remove the chicken and pour out all but 1 tbsp of the oil from the pot.
6. Add 1 medium onion (sliced), 2 cloves of garlic (crushed), and ¼ tsp salt, adding a little hot water if needed to deglaze the pot. Sauté until soft and golden.
7. Add the chicken back to the pot with 1 lb/450g baby new potatoes (washed and halved), 1 ¾ cups/400 ml chicken or vegetable stock, and 1 tsp Dijon mustard.
8. Stir, then place the lid on the Instant Pot, set valve to seal, select manual high pressure (pressure cook custom high on Evo Plus) for 15 minutes.
9. When Instant Pot beeps, allow 10 minutes before releasing the pressure.
10. When pin drops, open the lid. Press cancel.
11. Press the sauté button on the Instant Pot on normal heat, (custom level 3 for the Evo Plus).
12. Add 16 oz/400g of mixed spring vegetables (broccoli florets, peas, broad beans, and sliced courgette.
13. Select sauté as above, cook for 5 minutes or until vegetables are tender. Stir in 4 tbsp crème fraiche to make a creamy sauce, season with salt and pepper to taste.
14. Mix 2 tbsp cornstarch/cornflour with 2 tbsp cold water, stir in to thicken. Press cancel.
15. Add a handful of fresh tarragon leaves (roughly chopped), or ½ tsp of dried tarragon.

PREPARATION STEPS

1. Add ½ cup/125 ml olive oil, ¼ cup tomato paste/puree, ¼ cup lemon juice, 1 tsp garlic powder, 1 tsp onion powder, 1 tsp cumin powder, 1 tsp salt, 1 tsp freshly ground black pepper and 4 medium skinless, boneless chicken thighs about 1 lb/450g to a sealable food safe bag. Seal the bag and shake it well. Place in the refrigerator for at least 3 hours, overnight if possible.

2. Transfer the chicken and the marinade into the Instant Pot.

3. Place the lid on the Instant Pot, set valve to seal, select manual low pressure (pressure cook custom low on Evo Plus) for 8 minutes.

4. When Instant Pot beeps, allow 5 minutes before releasing the pressure.

5. Remove the chicken with a slotted spoon, reserve marinade, and cut or shred the chicken into small pieces.

6. Heat a large pan over a medium-high heat. Add 4 tbsp of the marinade, the chicken and 1 medium onion (sliced), season well. Cook for 4 to 5 minutes roasting to a rich dark color.

7. Alternatively, to sauté in the Instant Pot, cook in 2 batches. Press the sauté button on normal heat, (custom level 3 for the Evo Plus).

8. Once display says HOT, add 2 tbsp of the marinade, half of the chicken, and half of the onion, season well, cook for 4 to 5 minutes.

9. Set to one side, keep warm, and repeat with second batch.

10. Serve with toasted Pitta, salad, lemon slices, jalapenos, and garlic mayo.

Chicken Kebab (Shawarma)

Great street food at home.

SERVES 4

INGREDIENTS

- ½ cup/125 ml olive oil
- ¼ cup tomato paste/puree
- ¼ cup lemon juice
- 1 tsp garlic powder
- 1 tsp onion powder
- 1 tsp cumin powder
- 1 tsp salt
- 1 tsp freshly ground black pepper
- 4 medium skinless, boneless chicken thighs about 1 lb/450g
- 1 medium onion (sliced)

Shredded Chicken Burger

Sweet, smokey & satisfying.

SERVES 4

INGREDIENTS

- 2 tsp garlic powder
- ½ tsp ginger powder
- ½ tsp paprika
- 1 tsp smoked paprika
- ½ tsp mild chilli powder
- 2 tbsp dark brown sugar
- 1 tsp salt
- ½ tsp freshly ground black pepper
- 4 skinless, boneless chicken thighs
- 1 ½ tbsp olive oil
- ¾ cup/180 ml chicken stock
- 4 tbsp good barbeque sauce
- 1 tsp sriracha sauce
- 4 brioche buns
- Coleslaw to serve

PREPARATION STEPS

1. In a bowl, add 2 tsp garlic powder, ½ tsp ginger powder, ½ tsp paprika, 1 tsp smoked paprika, ½ tsp mild chilli powder, 2 tbsp dark brown sugar, 1 tsp salt, and ½ tsp freshly ground black pepper. Mix well.
2. Coat the chicken with the spice rub, cover, and place in the refrigerator for at least an hour.
3. Remove from the refrigerator 20 minutes before cooking, to bring to room temperature.
4. Press the sauté button on the Instant Pot on normal heat, (custom level 3 for the Evo Plus).
5. Once display says HOT, add 1 ½ tbsp of olive oil.
6. Add the chicken thighs, sauté for about 2 minutes on each side until golden.
7. Press cancel, add ¾ cup/180 ml chicken stock to the pot.
8. Place the lid on the Instant Pot, set valve to seal, select manual high pressure (pressure cook custom high on Evo Plus) for 10 minutes.
9. When Instant Pot beeps, allow 10 minutes before releasing the pressure.
10. When pin drops, open the lid, press cancel.
11. Remove the chicken from the pot, transfer to a chopping board.
12. Press the sauté button on the Instant Pot on normal heat, (custom level 3 for the Evo Plus), reduce the liquid for 5 to 6 minutes.
13. Shred the chicken into small pieces using two forks or a pair of kitchen scissors, return the shredded chicken to the pot.
14. Stir in 4 tbsp good barbeque sauce, and 1 tsp sriracha sauce.
15. Sauté for 2 to 3 minutes until the liquid has reduced and the sauce is sticky.
16. Heat a large pan over a medium high heat.
17. Cut, then toast the brioche buns face down in the pan for about 30 seconds or until golden.
18. Fill the buns with shredded chicken and salad, serve with coleslaw.
19. Also great with salad, rice or in a Tortilla wrap.

the chicken, place a lid on the bowl. Leave at room temperature while you prepare the other ingredients.
3. Cook 4 oz/115g smoked bacon (diced) in a large non-stick pan over a medium heat, stirring occasionally until brown and crisp. Transfer to a plate with a slotted spoon.
4. Add 8 oz/230g mushrooms to the bacon fat in the pan, season with salt. Cook, stirring occasionally until tender and golden brown. Place mushrooms into Instant Pot.
5. Remove chicken from marinade, pick out the thyme, set aside marinade. Pat chicken skin dry with paper towel.
6. Heat 2 tbsp unsalted butter in the pan over a medium heat, add chicken skin side down. Cook for 10 to 12 minutes undisturbed, until skin is dark golden brown and plenty of fat is rendered. Turn and cook the other side for about 2 minutes. Place chicken into Instant Pot.
7. Pour out oil from the pan, leaving about 1 tbsp.
8. Still on medium heat, add ¼ tsp baking soda, 8 oz/230g carrots, 4 shallots, and 2 smashed garlic cloves, season lightly with salt and freshly ground black pepper.
9. Cook stirring often until shallots are golden brown (about 4 minutes), add to Instant Pot, along with half of the reserved bacon.
10. Return pan to medium heat, pour in 2 tbsp of white wine vinegar. Simmer scraping up browned bits with a wooden spoon until syrupy, for about 1 minute. Add reserved wine marinade, remaining ½ bunch of thyme, and 1 tsp of vegetable bouillon. Bring to a simmer until reduced by half 5 to 7 minutes.
11. Pour liquid over chicken, place lid on Instant Pot, set valve to seal, select manual high pressure (pressure cook custom high on Evo Plus) for 15 minutes.
12. When Instant Pot beeps, allow 10 minutes natural pressure release, open the valve to release the rest of the pressure.
13. When pin drops, open the lid. Press cancel.
14. In a small bowl mix 1 tbsp all-purpose/plain flour and remaining 2 tablespoons of butter together well with a fork in a small bowl.
15. Transfer chicken legs and vegetables to a warm platter, leave liquid in pot. Pick out and discard thyme sprigs from liquid.
16. Press the sauté button on the Instant Pot on normal heat, (custom level 3 for the Evo Plus).
17. Whisk butter flour mixture into liquid. Bring to a simmer, cook to thicken sauce for about 3 minutes.
18. Taste and adjust seasoning if needed, stir in parsley.
19. Serve coq au vin with braising liquid poured over and all-around, sprinkle with remaining reserved bacon.

Coq au Vin

A classic French dish.

Perfect for the Instant Pot.

SERVES 4

INGREDIENTS

- 4 chicken legs (thigh and drumstick)
- Table salt and freshly ground black pepper to taste
- 2 cups/500 ml of dry white wine. one bunch of thyme (divided)
- 4 oz/115g smoked bacon (diced)
- 8 oz/230g mushrooms (your favourite variety)
- 4 tbsp unsalted butter
- ¼ tsp baking soda/sodium bicarbonate (not baking powder)
- 8 oz/230g carrots peeled and cut into 4 inch/10 cm pieces
- 4 peeled shallots
- 2 garlic cloves smashed
- 2 tbsp white wine vinegar
- 1 tbsp all-purpose/plain flour
- Handful of chopped parsley

PREPARATION STEPS

1. Pat chicken dry with paper towels, season well with table salt and freshly ground black pepper.
2. Place the 4 chicken legs into a large bowl, cover with 2 cups/500 ml of dry white wine, adding ½ of the bunch of thyme. Turn to coat

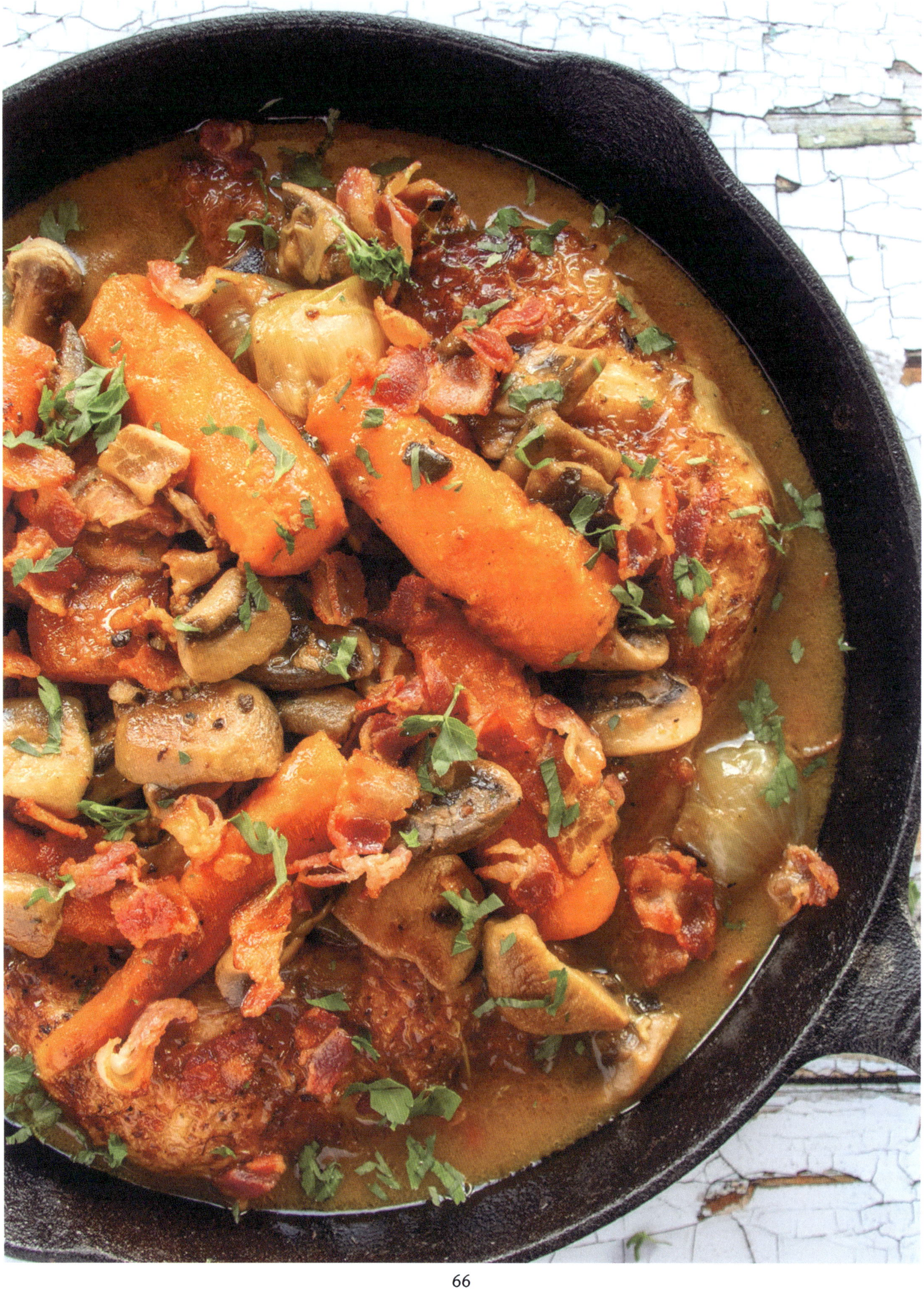

PREPARATION STEPS

1. Lay each chicken breast flat on a board lengthwise, with the thicker end of the breast at the top. Slice sideways into the breast from the top down making sure that the opposite side to the knife remains attached, so that the breast opens like a book when finished. (AKA butterflied)
2. Season the inside of the breast with a little salt.
3. Sandwich together one slice of ham and one slice of cheese, roll them up from one corner, place inside and close the breast.
4. Season well on both sides with salt and freshly ground black pepper.
5. Fill inner pot to just below maximum level with hot water.
6. Select sous vide mode custom 65 °/c/149 °/f, set time for 1 ½ hours.
7. Place chicken into a sous vide compatible zipper type bag, remove as much of the air as you can by lowering the bag into a bowl of water, using the water to push the air out of the bag, being careful not to allow any water into the bag. Seal while immersed or use a vacuum sealer.
8. Once up to temperature, lower the bag into the Instant Pot, close lid making sure valve is open.
9. A few minutes before the chicken is cooked, arrange three shallow trays next to each other, pour a cup of flour into one, 2 large, whisked eggs in the second, and in the third, a cup of panko breadcrumbs. Season all three with salt and freshly ground black pepper.
10. Pre heat a pan of oil, or a deep fat fryer to 210 °/c/410 °/f.
11. Remove the chicken from the bag, pat dry with a paper towel. Coat each one on both sides in the flour, then the eggs, and finally the panko breadcrumbs. (A great trick for this is to remember to keep one hand for the dry ingredients and the other for the egg).
12. Fry the chicken in the hot oil one or two pieces at a time, for a few seconds only, until the breadcrumbs turn golden brown. The chicken is already cooked, at these high temperatures it will only take a few seconds to brown, so don't take your eye off it, be ready to remove it with your slotted spoon.
13. Enjoy with your favourite sides.

Sous Vide Ham & Cheese Stuffed Chicken Breasts

Crispy and tender, the best of both worlds.

SERVES 4

INGREDIENTS

- 4 skinless boneless chicken breasts
- 4 squares pre sliced processed cheese (a flexible one that can be rolled up)
- 4 squares of pre sliced ham
- 1 cup panko breadcrumbs
- 1 cup plain/all-purpose flour
- 2 large eggs
- Salt & freshly ground black pepper to taste
- Vegetable oil (enough to cover chicken depending on pan size)

Sous Vide Piri Piri Chicken

Restaurant style tender sous vide chicken.

Excellent with rice and salad, or in a burger.

SERVES 2

INGREDIENTS

- 4 tbsp olive oil
- ½ red pepper (diced)
- 2 garlic cloves (crushed)
- 1 tbsp white wine vinegar
- 1-2 chilli peppers
- ½ tsp salt
- 1 tsp dried oregano
- 2 tbsp lemon juice
- 2 tbsp water
- 2 skinless boneless chicken breasts

PREPARATION STEPS

1. Press the sauté button on the Instant Pot on normal heat, (custom level 3 for the Evo Plus).
2. Once display says HOT, add 4 tbsp of the olive oil.
3. Add ½ red pepper (diced), sauté for 3-4 minutes until the pepper begins to soften.
4. Add 2 garlic cloves (crushed), sauté for 1 minute.
5. Add 1 tbsp white wine vinegar, 1-2 chilli peppers, ½ tsp salt, and 1 tsp dried oregano.
6. Press cancel, remove inner pot, and stir the mixture.
7. Add 2 tbsp lemon juice, and 2 tbsp water, allow the mixture to cool slightly.
8. Pour the mix into a blender and blitz for 30 seconds, or until smooth.
9. Clean the inner pot, then fill to just below maximum with hot water.
10. Select sous vide mode custom 65 °/c/149 °/f, set time for 1 ½ hours and bring up to temperature.
11. Add 2 skinless boneless chicken breasts and the mixture to to a sous vide compatible zipper type bag.
12. Remove as much of the air as you can by lowering the bag into a bowl of water, using the water to push the air out of the bag, being careful not to allow any water into the bag. Seal while immersed or use a vacuum sealer.
13. After 1 ½ hours, remove bag, empty and dry inner pot.
14. Pour the liquid from the bag into the inner pot, remove the chicken from the bag, pat dry with kitchen towel, and place on a heat proof trivet or rack in a heat proof tray.
15. Press the sauté button on the Instant Pot on normal heat, (custom level 3 for the Evo Plus).
16. Reduce the liquid, whisking until the Piri Piri sauce is smooth and desired thickness is reached.
17. Press cancel, remove inner pot.
18. In heat safe place on a wire rack, using a kitchen blowtorch, sear the chicken all over until charred.
19. Slice the chicken and serve with the Piri Piri sauce.
20. Serve with rice, salad, or in a toasted burger.

Fish

Smokey fish Stew

Fresh and tasty.

SERVES 4

INGREDIENTS

- 1 handful of fresh parsley (finely chopped)
- 2 garlic cloves (finely chopped)
- 1 lemon (zest & juice)
- 4 tbsp olive oil
- 1 red onion (finely sliced)
- 1 lb/450g new potatoes (quartered)
- 1 red chilli (finely chopped)
- 2 tsp fennel seeds
- ½ tsp salt
- ¼ tsp black pepper
- 1 tsp smoked paprika
- 1 x 14 oz/400g can chopped tomatoes
- ½ cup/125ml fish stock
- ½ cup 125ml white wine
- 1 x 14 oz/400g can chickpeas (drained)
- 1 lb/450g mixed fresh fish (cut in chunks)
- 7 oz/200g raw shrimp/prawns
- 3 cups/400g mussels

PREPARATION STEPS

1. In a small bowl mix 1 handful of flat leaf parsley (finely chopped), 1 of the garlic cloves (finely chopped), zest of 1 lemon and 1 tbsp of the olive oil. Reserve for later.

2. Press the sauté button on the Instant Pot on normal heat, (custom level 3 for the Evo Plus).

3. Once display says HOT, add 2 tbsp of the olive oil.

4. Add 1 red onion (finely sliced) and 1 lb/450g new potatoes (quartered), stir regularly for 5 minutes.

5. Add the last 1 tbsp olive oil, 1 garlic clove (finely chopped), 1 red chilli (finely chopped), 2 tsp fennel seeds, ½ tsp salt, and ¼ tsp freshly ground black pepper, cook for 1 minute.

6. Add 1 tsp smoked paprika, juice of 1 lemon, 1 x 14 oz/400g can chopped tomatoes, ½ cup/125 ml fish stock, ½ cup/125 ml white wine, and 1 x 14 oz/400g can chickpeas (drained). Stir then press cancel.

7. Place the lid on the Instant Pot, set valve to seal, select manual high pressure (pressure cook custom high on Evo Plus) for 12 minutes.

8. When Instant Pot beeps, quick release the pressure.

9. When pin drops, open the lid.

10. Add 1 lb/450g mixed fresh fish (cut in chunks), raw shrimp/prawns and 3 cups/400g of mussels, carefully check they are all closed before cooking, and all open after cooking, discard any that are not.

11. Place the lid on the Instant Pot, set valve to seal, select manual low pressure (pressure cook custom low on Evo Plus) for 2 minutes.

12. When Instant Pot beeps, quick release the pressure.

13. When pin drops, open the lid. Press cancel.

14. Stir in reserved parsley, garlic, lemon zest and olive oil dressing from step 1.

15. Check seasoning and serve.

PLEASE DO NOT MAKE THIS AGAIN. HORRIBLE!

Tuna & Tomato Penne

A quick and tasty weekday pasta.

SERVES 4

Blurgh

INGREDIENTS

- 2 tbsp olive oil
- 1 medium red onion (finely sliced)
- 1 fresh red chilli (finely sliced)
- 1 small bunch fresh basil (stalks finely sliced & leaves reserved)
- ½ tsp ground cinnamon
- 1 x 14 oz/400g can tuna in oil (drained)
- 1 x 14 oz/400g can diced tomatoes
- 2 cups/200g dried penne
- 2 ½ cups/ 600 ml boiling water
- 1 lemon
- ½ cup/40g Parmesan cheese
- ¾ tsp salt
- ¾ tsp freshly ground black pepper

PREPARATION STEPS

1. Peel and finely slice 1 medium red onion, 1 fresh red chilli, and the stalks from the small bunch of fresh basil (reserve leaves for later).
2. Press the sauté button on the Instant Pot on normal heat, (custom level 3 for the Evo Plus) once display says HOT, add 2 tbsp of olive oil.
3. Add 1 medium red onion, 1 fresh red chilli, 1 small bunch fresh basil, and ½ tsp ground cinnamon.
4. Sauté for about 7 minutes stirring regularly.
5. Once the onions are starting to brown, add 1 x 14 oz/400g can tuna in oil (drained), 1 x 14 oz/400g can diced tomatoes, 2 ½ cups/600ml boiling water, ¾ tsp salt and ¾ tsp freshly ground black pepper.
6. Stir in 2 cup/200g dried penne pasta.
7. Press cancel, place lid on Instant Pot, set valve to seal, select manual high pressure (pressure cook custom high on Evo Plus) 2 minutes.
8. When Instant Pot beeps, allow 5 minutes natural pressure release then open the valve to release the rest of the pressure. Press cancel.
9. Taste and season if needed.
10. Grate in the zest and juice of 1 small lemon and half the Parmesan. Stir in.
11. Serve topped with basil leaves and the remaining Parmesan.

Sous Vide Tuna Confit

So much better than canned.

SERVES 4

INGREDIENTS

- 8 oz/230g tuna steak (roughly 3 inch/7.5 cm wide x 1 inch/2.5 cm thick)
- Salt (to taste)
- Good olive oil

PREPARATION STEPS

1. Sprinkle each steak generously with salt on all sides, place the steak on a plate in a refrigerator for 20 minutes.

2. Fill inner pot to ¾ full with hot water. Select sous vide mode custom 50 °/c/121 °/f, set time for 30 minutes and bring up to temperature.

3. After 20 minutes, rinse the excess salt off the tuna and blot the pieces dry with paper towels. Place the tuna in a sous vide compatible zipper type bag as evenly as you can, then add enough olive oil to just submerge the tuna when you hold the bag by its upper corners.

4. Remove as much of the air as you can by lowering the bag into a bowl of water, using the water to push the air out of the bag, being careful not to allow any water into the bag. Seal while immersed or use a vacuum sealer.

5. Once up to temperature, cook for 30 minutes.

6. When cooked, remove from water bath. Eat whilst still warm or place the bag into an ice bath for 15 minutes to chill.

7. Store in the refrigerator and eat within two days.

Salads

Thai Chicken & Mango Salad

A beautifully refreshing salad that has it all, sweet, sour, bitter, salty & umami.

Best enjoyed outside in the sunshine.

SERVES 2

INGREDIENTS

Main Dish

- 4 boneless chicken thighs (skin on)
- Salt
- Freshly ground black pepper
- 1 tbsp olive oil
- 4 tbsp Thai fish sauce
- 4 tbsp golden caster sugar
- 1.5 tbsp lime juice
- 1.5 inch/4 cm fresh root ginger (peeled and grated)
- 2 red Thai chillies (chopped)
- ¼ cup/60 ml hot water

Salad

- 2 tbsp olive oil
- 8 banana shallots (peeled and sliced)
- 1 mango (ripe)
- 2 red chillies (seeded and cut into thin strips)
- 1 small bunch of fresh cilantro/coriander leaves
- 1 small bunch of fresh mint leaves
- Juice of 2 limes
- 2 tbsp Thai fish sauce
- 1 tsp caster sugar

PREPARATION STEPS

1. Season 4 boneless chicken thighs (skin on) with salt and freshly ground black pepper.
2. Press the sauté button on the Instant Pot on normal heat, (custom level 3 for the Evo Plus).
3. Add 1 tbsp olive oil to the pot. Once HOT is displayed, add the chicken and sauté for about 5 minutes skin side down, turn over and repeat for about 2 minutes.
4. Add 4 tbsp Thai fish sauce, 4 tbsp golden caster sugar, 1.5 tbsp lime juice, 1.5 inch/4 cm fresh root ginger (peeled and grated), 2 red Thai chillies (chopped) and ¼ cup/60 ml of hot water.
5. Place the lid on the Instant Pot, set valve to seal, select manual high pressure (pressure cook custom high on Evo Plus) for 10 minutes.
6. When Instant Pot beeps, allow 5 minutes natural pressure release. Press cancel. Set the chicken to one side in a bowl, leaving the sauce in the pot.
7. Press the sauté button on the Instant Pot on high heat, (custom level 6 for the Evo Plus).
8. Reduce the sauce by about two thirds, pour over the chicken to coat. Press cancel, clean the pot.
9. Press the sauté button on the Instant Pot on normal heat, (custom level 3 for the Evo Plus) once display says HOT, add 2 tbsp of olive oil.
10. Add two thirds of the 8 banana shallots (peeled and sliced).
11. Sauté them for five minutes, or until crisp and golden, turn them out onto a sheet of paper towel to cool and drain.
12. Peel the mango, then slice each of the cheeks from the stone in the centre. Slice the mango flesh into long thin slivers and place them into a bowl with the remaining uncooked shallots. Add 2 red chillies (seeded and cut into thin strips), 1 small bunch of fresh cilantro/coriander leaves and 1 small bunch of fresh mint leaves.
13. In a smaller bowl make the dressing, mix the juice of 2 limes, 2 tbsp Thai fish sauce and 1 tsp caster sugar.
14. Toss the salad, add dressing to taste, divide salad between 2 plates.
15. Slice the chicken and place a few slices on each plate. Sprinkle with some of the crispy shallots, drizzle the remaining sauce over the chicken and serve.

PREPARATION STEPS

1. Add 1 cup/250 ml of cold water and the trivet to the pot, distribute 1.3 lb/600g new potatoes (scrubbed and cut into 1 inch/2.5 cm pieces) and 3 large eggs (room temperature) into a steamer basket, in the Instant Pot.

2. Place the lid on the Instant Pot, set valve to seal, select manual high pressure (pressure cook custom high on Evo Plus) for 7 minutes.

3. In the meantime, in a serving bowl mix 1.4 oz/40g green/spring onions (finely sliced), 4 tbsp mayonnaise, 2 tsp white wine vinegar, ½ tsp salt, and ¼ tsp freshly ground black pepper. Reserve in the fridge.

4. When Instant Pot beeps, quick release the pressure.

5. When pin drops, open the lid. Press cancel.

6. Remove eggs, leave them in ice water then set aside, allow potatoes and eggs to cool.

7. Once cooled, add potatoes to serving bowl, gently stir in the dressing with a spatula to coat potatoes.

8. Peel boiled eggs (easiest to peel under running water) then quarter. Add to serving bowl, gently stir in with spatula. Adjust seasoning to taste, serve garnished with fresh chives.

Potato & Egg Salad

A perfect side dish for a picnic or barbecue.

SERVES 6

INGREDIENTS

- 1 cup/250 ml cold water for steaming
- 1.3 lb/600g new potatoes (scrubbed and cut into ¾ inch/2 cm pieces)
- 3 large eggs (room temperature)
- 1.4 oz/40g green/spring onions (finely sliced)
- 4 tbsp mayonnaise
- 2 tsp white wine vinegar
- ½ tsp salt
- ¼ tsp freshly ground black pepper
- A few freshly cut chives for garnish

Coronation Chicken

Delicious in a sandwich, with rice or on a baked potato.

SERVES 4

INGREDIENTS

- 1 cup/250 ml water (for pressure)
- 1 lb/450g skinless chicken breasts
- 1 ½ tbsp olive oil
- 1 small onion (finely chopped)
- 1 tbsp curry powder
- 1 tbsp tomato paste/puree
- ½ cup red wine
- 2 tsp lemon juice
- 1 bay leaf
- ¼ tsp salt
- ¼ tsp freshly ground black pepper
- 1 ½ tbsp mango chutney
- 2/3 cup/80g mayonnaise
- 2/3/ cup/80g crème fraiche
- ¼ cup sultanas
- 1 small handful fresh cilantro/coriander leaves (chopped)

PREPARATION STEPS

1. Add 1 cup/250 ml of water and the trivet to the pot, place 1 lb/450g skinless chicken breasts onto the trivet.
2. Place the lid on the Instant Pot, set valve to seal, select manual high pressure (pressure cook custom high on Evo Plus) for 10 minutes.
3. When Instant Pot beeps, allow 10 minutes before releasing the pressure.
4. When pin drops, open the lid. Press cancel.
5. Set chicken to one side to cool, discard water and clean inner pot.
6. Press the sauté button on the Instant Pot on normal heat, (custom level 3 for the Evo Plus).
7. Once display says HOT, add 1 ½ tbsp olive oil and 1 small onion (finely chopped) to the pot, sauté for 3 minutes stirring regularly.
8. Add 1 tbsp curry powder, sauté for 20 seconds stirring constantly.
9. Add 1 tbsp tomato paste/puree, ½ cup red wine, 2 tsp lemon juice, 1 bay leaf, ¼ tsp salt, and ¼ tsp freshly ground black pepper, sauté for 3 minutes stirring occasionally.
10. Transfer to a large bowl and allow to cool. Press cancel.
11. Slice reserved chicken into ½ inch/1 to 2 cm pieces.
12. Once mixture is cool, remove bay leaf, add reserved chicken, 1 ½ tbsp mango chutney, 2/3 cup/80g mayonnaise, 2/3 cup/80g crème fraiche, and ¼ cup sultanas. Mix thoroughly.
13. Scatter 1 small handful of fresh chopped cilantro/coriander leaves to serve.

Vegetarian

Zucchini/Courgette & Cauliflower Curry

A clean and simple curry.

SERVES 4

INGREDIENTS

- 2 tbsp olive oil
- ½ tsp cumin seeds
- 2 onions (chopped)
- 4 garlic cloves (crushed)
- 1 inch/2.5 cm ginger (chopped)
- ½ tsp turmeric
- 1 tsp Kashmiri chilli powder
- 1 tbsp dried curry leaves
- 1 tsp Madras curry powder
- 1 tsp garam masala
- 1 tsp salt
- ½ tsp freshly ground black pepper
- 1 cauliflower (cut into florets)
- 1 zucchini/courgette (diced)
- 17oz/500g coconut cream
- ½ cup water
- 1 handful fresh cilantro/coriander (finely chopped)

PREPARATION STEPS

1. Press the sauté button on the Instant Pot on normal heat, (custom level 3 for the Evo Plus).
2. Once display says HOT, add 2 tbsp of olive oil.
3. Sauté ½ tsp cumin seeds, 2 onions (chopped), 4 garlic cloves (crushed), and 1 inch/2.5 cm ginger (chopped). Stir regularly for 5 minutes.
4. Add ½ tsp turmeric, 1 tsp Kashmiri chilli powder, 1 tbsp dried curry leaves, 1 tsp Madras curry powder, 1 tsp garam masala, 1 tsp salt and ½ tsp freshly ground black pepper, saute for 20 seconds stirring constantly.
5. Add 1 cauliflower (cut into florets), 1 zucchini/courgette (diced), 17 oz/500g coconut cream, and ½ cup water. Stir to combine. Press cancel.
6. Place the lid on the Instant Pot, set valve to seal, select manual high pressure (pressure cook custom high on Evo Plus) for 1 minute.
7. When Instant Pot beeps, quick release the pressure. Press cancel.
8. When pin drops, open the lid.
9. Stir through 1 handful fresh cilantro/coriander (finely chopped).

PREPARATION STEPS

1. Press the sauté button on the Instant Pot on normal heat, (custom level 3 for the Evo Plus).

2. Once display says HOT, add 1 tbsp of olive oil, 1 onion (diced), 2 garlic cloves (crushed) and 1 butternut squash (peeled and cut into approx ½ inch/1cm cubes).

3. Sauté for 3 minutes. Press cancel.

4. Stir in ¾ cup/120g pearl barley (rinsed), ¾ cup/140g dried green lentils (rinsed), 3 cups/720 ml vegetable stock, 2/3 cup/160 ml white wine, 1 tsp salt and ½ tsp freshly ground black pepper.

5. Place the lid on the Instant Pot, set valve to seal, select manual low pressure (pressure cook custom low on Evo Plus) for 25 minutes.

6. When Instant Pot beeps, press cancel. Quick release the pressure.

7. When pin drops, open the lid, let stand for 5 minutes then serve.

8. If it's Halloween…. try serving it in a pumpkin.

Scary Squash Risotto

Scarily tasty.

SERVES 6

INGREDIENTS

- 1 tbsp olive oil
- 1 onion (diced)
- 2 garlic cloves (crushed)
- 1 butternut squash (peeled and cut into approx ½ inch/1cm cubes)
- ¾ cup/120g pearl barley (rinsed)
- ¾ cup/140g dried green lentils (rinsed)
- 3 cups/720 ml vegetable stock
- 2/3 cup/160 ml white wine
- 1 tsp salt
- ½ tsp freshly ground black pepper

Black Bean Chilli

Quick healthy and tasty dinner.

SERVES 4

INGREDIENTS

- 1 red onion (finely chopped)
- 4 cloves garlic (crushed)
- 1 red & 1 yellow bell pepper (roughly sliced)
- 1 fresh chilli (finely sliced)
- 2 leeks (roughly chopped)
- 2 tbsp olive oil
- 1 tsp cumin seeds
- 2 tsp salt
- 1 x 14 oz/400g can black beans (drained and rinsed)
- 2 x 14 oz/400g cans chopped tomatoes
- ½ cup/125g tomato paste/puree
- 1 tsp ground cilantro/coriander
- 1 tsp ground cumin
- ¼ tsp smoked paprika
- ¼ tsp freshly ground black pepper
- 1 tbsp honey (or preferred sweetener)
- 1 handful fresh cilantro/coriander (finely chopped)
- Juice of ½ a lime

PREPARATION STEPS

1. Peel and finely chop 1 red onion and crush 4 cloves of garlic.
2. De-seed and roughly slice 1 red and 1 yellow bell pepper, finely slice the red chilli.
3. Trim and roughly chop 2 leeks.
4. Press the sauté button on the Instant Pot on normal heat, (custom level 3 for the Evo Plus).
5. Once display says HOT, add 2 tbsp of olive oil.
6. Sauté the onion and garlic for about 5 minutes, stirring regularly.
7. Add 1 red and 1 yellow bell pepper (roughly sliced), 1 fresh chilli (finely sliced), 2 leeks (roughly chopped), 1 tsp cumin seeds, and 2 tsp salt.
8. Sauté for another 3 minutes.
9. Add 1 x 14 oz/400g can black beans (drained and rinsed), 2 x 14 oz/400g cans chopped tomatoes, ½ cup/125g tomato paste/puree, 1 tsp ground cilantro/coriander, 1 tsp ground cumin, ¼ tsp smoked paprika, ¼ tsp freshly ground black pepper, and 1 tbsp honey (or preferred sweetener). Press cancel.
10. Place the lid on the Instant Pot, set valve to seal, select manual low pressure (pressure cook custom low on Evo Plus) for 3 minutes.
11. When Instant Pot beeps, quick release the pressure.
12. When pin drops, open the lid. Press cancel.
13. Stir through 1 handful fresh cilantro/coriander (finely chopped) and the juice of ½ a lime.

PREPARATION STEPS

1. Place 11oz/300g tomatoes (quartered) into a colander, sprinkle ½ tsp salt on the tomatoes whilst tossing them, allow them to drain over a bowl for 20 minutes.
2. Press the sauté button on the Instant Pot on normal heat, (custom level 3 for the Evo Plus).
3. Once display says HOT, add 2 tbsp of olive oil.
4. Add 1 medium onion (diced) and 2 garlic cloves (crushed).
5. Sauté for 3–4 minutes stirring regularly.
6. Add 1 red bell pepper (cut into 1 inch/2 -3 cm pieces), 1 tbsp mixed dried herbs, 1 tsp salt, ¼ tsp freshly ground black pepper and the drained tomatoes.
7. Cook for 2 minutes stirring regularly.
8. Stir in 1 medium eggplant/aubergine (cut into 1 inch/2 -3 cm pieces) and 1 medium zucchini/courgette (cut into 1 inch/2-3 cm pieces). Press cancel.
9. Place the lid on the Instant Pot, set valve to seal, select manual low pressure (pressure cook custom low on Evo Plus) for 5 minutes.
10. When Instant Pot beeps, quick release pressure.
11. When pin drops, open the lid.
12. Sprinkle ratatouille with grated Parmesan cheese and freshly ground black pepper.
13. Serve with roasted meat, fish, or freshly baked bread.

Ratatouille

A classic.

SERVES 4

INGREDIENTS

- 11 oz/300g tomatoes (quartered)
- ½ tsp salt (for draining tomatoes)
- 2 tbsp olive oil
- 1 medium onion (diced)
- 2 garlic cloves (crushed)
- 1 red bell pepper (cut into 1 inch/2-3 cm pieces)
- 1 tbsp mixed dried herbs
- 1 tsp salt
- ¼ tsp freshly ground black pepper
- 1 medium eggplant/aubergine (cut into 1 inch/2-3 cm pieces)
- 1 medium zucchini/courgette (cut into 1 inch/2-3 cm pieces)
- Parmesan cheese to taste

Thai Green Tofu Curry

Perfect with coconut rice.

SERVES 4

INGREDIENTS

- 2 tbsp olive oil
- 14 oz/400g firm tofu (not silken) cubed 1 inch/ 2.5 cm
- 1 onion (chopped)
- 3 garlic cloves (crushed)
- 1 inch/2.5 cm ginger (peeled and grated)
- 1 handful fresh cilantro/coriander stalks
- 3 tbsp green curry paste
- 2 x 14 oz/400ml cans coconut milk
- 2 green birdseye chillies (halved lengthways)
- 4 tbsp tamari/soy sauce
- Zest of 1 lime
- 4 small potatoes (unpeeled, quartered)
- 2 medium carrots (peeled and sliced lengthways)
- 1 handful green beans (trimmed)
- 1 green bell pepper (sliced)
- 2 handfuls of spinach
- 1 handful fresh coriander leaves
- 1 ½ tbsp cornstarch/cornflour
- 1 ½ tbsp cold water

PREPARATION STEPS

1. Cut 14 oz/400g firm tofu (not silken) into 1 inch/ 2.5 cm pieces (use paper towel to absorb any excess moisture).

2. Heat a <u>non-stick</u> pan on medium heat. Once hot, add 1 tbsp of the olive oil, sauté gently turning for 5 minutes until golden on all sides, remove and set aside.

3. Press the sauté button on the Instant Pot on normal heat, (custom level 3 for the Evo Plus).

4. Once display says HOT, add the rest of the oil along with 1 onion (chopped), 3 garlic cloves (crushed), 1 inch/2.5 cm ginger (peeled and grated) and 1 handful of fresh coriander stalks. Cook for 2 minutes, stirring regularly.

5. Add 3 tbsp green curry paste, cook for another minute. Stir regularly.

6. Add 2 x 14 oz/400 ml cans coconut milk, 2 green birdseye chillies (halved lengthways), 4 tbsp tamari/soy sauce, zest of 1 lime, 4 small potatoes (unpeeled, quartered), and 2 medium carrots (peeled and sliced lengthways). Stir then press cancel.

7. Place the lid on the Instant Pot, set valve to seal, select manual high pressure (pressure cook custom high on Evo Plus) for 10 minutes.

8. When Instant Pot beeps, quick release the pressure.

9. When pin drops, open the lid. Press cancel.

10. Press sauté as above, add 1 handful green beans (trimmed), cook for 4 minutes, then add 1 green bell pepper (sliced), cook for another 3 minutes, stirring occasionally.

11. Mix 1 ½ tbsp cornstarch/cornflour with 1 ½ tbsp cold water in a cup, stir in to thicken. Press cancel.

12. Stir in reserved tofu, 2 handfuls of spinach and 1 handful fresh coriander leaves.

PREPARATION STEPS

1. Add 1 cup/250 ml of water for pressure and your trivet to the pot.
2. Wash and add 1 lb/450g whole sweet potatoes (2 inches/5 cm or less in width).
3. Place lid on Instant Pot, set valve to seal, select manual high pressure (pressure cook custom high on Evo Plus) for 15 minutes.
4. When Instant Pot beeps, allow 10 minutes before releasing the pressure.
5. When pin drops, open the lid. Press cancel.
6. Place the sweet potatoes on a rack to cool. Discard the water and clean the pot.
7. Once cooled, halve the potatoes, and scoop out the inside into a bowl with a spoon.
8. Add 1 x 14 oz/400g can black beans (drained and rinsed) to the bowl, mash gently leaving some beans whole.
9. Press the sauté button on the Instant Pot on normal heat, (custom level 3 for the Evo Plus).
10. Once display says HOT, add 1 tbsp olive oil, ½ tsp cumin seeds, 1 medium red onion (finely chopped), 1 red chilli (finely chopped) and 1 clove garlic (finely chopped).
11. Sauté for 3 minutes, stirring regularly.
12. Stir in 1 tsp garam masala, 1 tsp Madras curry powder, ¼ cup fresh cilantro/coriander (chopped), 1 tsp salt, and ½ tsp freshly ground black pepper. Press cancel.
13. Incorporate this mixture into the bowl of sweet potato, divide the into 4 equal sized balls, then press and mould these into burger shapes.
14. Pour 1 ½ cups/100g panko breadcrumbs into a tray, place the burgers into the breadcrumbs, to coat all sides.
15. Mix ¼ cup/60 ml cold water, 3 tbsp cornstarch/flour, and 3 tbsp all-purpose/plain flour together in a bowl.
16. Coat the burgers in the slurry then give them a second coat in the breadcrumbs.
17. Press the sauté button on the Instant Pot on normal heat, (custom level 3 for the Evo Plus).
18. Give the burgers a good coating of spray cooking oil.
19. Once display says HOT, add the burgers and sauté for five minutes on each side, or until golden.

Spiced Sweet Potato Burger

A heavenly tasting burger.

SERVES 4

INGREDIENTS

- 1 cup/250 ml of water for pressure
- 1 lb/450g whole sweet potatoes (2 inches/5 cm or less in width)
- 1 x 14 oz/400g can black beans (drained and rinsed)
- 1 tbsp olive oil. ½ tsp cumin seeds
- 1 medium red onion (finely chopped)
- 1 red chilli (finely chopped)
- 1 clove garlic (finely chopped)
- 1 tsp garam masala
- 1 tsp Madras curry powder
- ¼ cup fresh cilantro/coriander (chopped)
- 1 tsp salt
- ½ tsp freshly ground black pepper
- 1 ½ cups/100g panko breadcrumbs
- ¼ cup/60 ml cold water
- 3 tbsp cornstarch/flour
- 3 tbsp all-purpose/plain flour
- Spray cooking oil

Cheese & Leek Galette

Simple and tasty.

SERVES 4

INGREDIENTS

- 1 tbsp unsalted butter
- 1 cup/100g leeks (sliced)
- 1 cup/250 ml cold water for steaming
- 1 cup/150g potatoes (peeled and cut into ¾ inch/2 cm pieces)
- ¼ cup/20g mushrooms (sliced)
- ¼ cup/50g cherry tomatoes (halved)
- 1 tsp dried mixed herbs
- ½ tsp salt
- ½ tsp freshly ground black pepper
- 1 cup/80g cheddar (grated)
- 1 lb/450g pre-made short crust pastry
- All-purpose/plain flour (for dusting)
- 1 egg yolk
- 1 tbsp milk

PREPARATION STEPS

1. Press the sauté button on the Instant Pot on normal heat, (custom level 3 for the Evo Plus).
2. Once display says HOT, add 1 tbsp unsalted butter and 1 cup/100g of leeks (sliced) to the pot.
3. Sauté until soft then reserve. Clean inner pot.
4. Place steamer basket, trivet and 1 cup/250 ml cold water into the pot. Add 1 cup/150g of potatoes (peeled and cut into ¾ inch/2 cm pieces) into a steamer basket.
5. Place the lid on the Instant Pot, set valve to seal, select manual high pressure (pressure cook custom high on Evo Plus) for 7 minutes.
6. When Instant Pot beeps, quick release the pressure.
7. When pin drops, open the lid. Press cancel. Allow the potatoes to cool for 10 minutes.
8. Add the potatoes, leek, ¼ cup/20g mushrooms (sliced), ¼ cup/50g cherry tomatoes (halved), 1 tsp dried mixed herbs, ½ tsp salt and ½ tsp freshly ground black pepper to a bowl. Gently combine.
9. Place 1 lb/450g of pre-made short crust pastry onto a baking parchment. Lightly flour the surface of both the parchment and the dough. Roll out the dough into a 10 inch/25 cm round circle, ¼ of an inch/ 0.6 cm thick. Place the filling in the middle of the circle and sprinkle 1 cup/80g of cheddar on top. Fold up the sides of the dough and press into the filling to secure. Lift the parchment paper and galette, place onto a baking tray.
10. In a small bowl, whisk the egg yolk and 1 tbsp milk. Brush the pastry with the wash, then place the baking tray into the oven and bake for 20 minutes 350 °/f/180 °/c or until the crust has turned golden brown.
11. Serve with fresh greens.

PREPARATION STEPS

1. Add 2 cups/200g preferred pasta, pinch of salt, cold water (approx. 2 cups/500 ml (enough to just cover pasta) and 2 large broccoli heads (cut into florets) to the pot.

2. Place lid on Instant Pot, set valve to seal, select manual high pressure (pressure cook custom high on Evo Plus) 2 minutes.

3. In the meantime, combine 1 tsp lemon zest, 2 tbsp lemon juice, 3 tbsp extra virgin olive oil, ¼ cup/25g parmesan (finely grated), 1 garlic clove (minced), ½ tsp mixed dried herbs, ½ tsp chilli flakes, ½ tsp sugar, ½ tsp salt and ½ tsp freshly ground black pepper in a bowl.

4. When Instant Pot beeps, press cancel and allow 5 minutes natural pressure release, then open the valve to release the rest of the pressure. Press cancel.

5. Take the lid off the pot, stir the mixture into the pasta, with 1 cup/100g grated cheddar.

6. Garnish with Parmesan add salt and freshly ground black pepper to taste.

7. Serve immediately.

Broccoli Cheese Pasta

A tasty and quick main or side dish.

SERVES 4

INGREDIENTS

- 2 cups/200g preferred pasta
- Pinch of salt
- 2 cups/500 ml cold water (enough to just cover pasta)
- 2 large broccoli heads (cut into florets)
- 1 tsp lemon zest
- 2 tbsp lemon juice
- 3 tbsp extra virgin olive oil
- ¼ cup/25g parmesan (finely grated)
- 1 garlic clove (minced)
- ½ tsp mixed dried herbs
- ½ tsp chilli flakes
- ½ tsp sugar
- ½ tsp salt
- ½ tsp freshly ground black pepper
- 1 cup/100g grated cheddar
- Parmesan to garnish

Simple Pesto Pasta

Basic & easy "no need to drain" pasta.

SERVES 4

INGREDIENTS

- 2 cups/200g preferred pasta
- Pinch of salt
- 2 cups/500 ml cold water (enough to just cover pasta)
- ½ cup/100g of your favorite pesto

PREPARATION STEPS

1. Add all the ingredients (except the pesto) to the pot.

2. Place lid on Instant Pot, set valve to seal, select manual high pressure (pressure cook custom high on Evo Plus) 2 minutes.

3. When Instant Pot beeps, allow 5 minutes natural pressure release, then open the valve to release the rest of the pressure. Press cancel.

4. Stir in ½ cup/100g of your favorite pesto.

5. Enjoy as a side, or cold in a lunch box.

Sides

Mash in a Flash

The fastest mash in the West.

3 minutes cook time.

Dairy free.

SERVES 4

INGREDIENTS

- 1.5 lb/700g diced potato (washed and peeled approx
- ½ inch/1 cm)
- 2 cups/500 ml boiling water
- 1 tsp salt
- 2 tbsp olive oil
- 1 tbsp whole grain mustard
- Fresh chives (finely chopped) to taste

PREPARATION STEPS

1. Boil 2 cups/500 ml of water.
2. Whilst the water is heating, prepare 1.5 lb/700g diced potato (washed and peeled approx. ½ inch/1 cm).
3. Add the water, potatoes, and 1 tsp of salt to the pot.
4. Place the lid on the Instant Pot, set valve to seal, select manual high pressure (pressure cook custom high on Evo Plus) for 3 minutes.
5. When Instant Pot beeps, quick release the pressure.
6. When pin drops, open the lid. Press cancel.
7. Remove inner pot, drain the potatoes in a colander, then add them back to the inner pot, place on a towel or heat proof surface.
8. Mash, adding 2 tbsp of olive oil.
9. Once mashed, stir in 1 tbsp whole grain mustard, a few fresh finely chopped chives and salt to taste.

PREPARATION STEPS

1. Add 2 cups/500 ml of water, 2 garlic cloves (finely chopped), 1 ¼ tsp salt, and 4 cups/500g frozen peas to the pot.
2. Place the lid on the Instant Pot, set valve to seal, select manual high pressure (pressure cook custom high on Evo Plus) for 3 minutes.
3. When Instant Pot beeps, quick release the pressure.
4. When pin drops, open the lid. Press cancel.
5. Remove the inner pot and drain the water from the peas in a colander.
6. Place the inner pot back into the Instant Pot to keep warm.
7. Place the drained peas back in the pot, add 1 ½ tbsp unsalted butter, stir with a spatula and use a potato masher to gently mash the peas.
8. Add 2 tbsp crème fraiche, 1 small handful fresh mint (finely chopped), ¼ tsp salt, and ¼ tsp freshly ground black pepper. Add lemon juice or vinegar to taste (optional).
9. Give it all a good stir with a spatula then serve immediately whilst still hot.

Crushed Peas with Mint & Creme Fraiche

Perfect with homemade fish and chips.

SERVES 4

INGREDIENTS

- 2 cups/500 ml water
- 2 garlic cloves (finely chopped)
- 1 ¼ tsp salt
- 4 cups/500g frozen peas
- 1 ½ tbsp unsalted butter
- 2 tbsp crème fraiche
- 1 small handful fresh mint (finely chopped)
- ¼ tsp freshly ground black pepper
- Lemon juice or vinegar to taste (optional)

Crunchy Cauliflower Cheese

Always a great little side dish.

SERVES 4

INGREDIENTS

Breadcrumb Mix

- 1 tbsp olive oil
- ½ cup/30g panko breadcrumbs
- ¼ tsp salt
- ¼ tsp freshly ground black pepper
- ¼ tsp cayenne pepper
- 1 cup of water (for pressure)
- 1 cauliflower (cut into florets)

Sauce

- 3 ½ tbsp unsalted butter
- 1/3 cup/45g all-purpose/plain flour
- 2 cups/500 ml milk
- 1 cup/100g grated cheddar
- 1 tsp of your favourite mustard
- ¼ tsp salt
- ¼ tsp freshly ground black pepper

PREPARATION STEPS

1. Press the sauté button on the Instant Pot on normal heat, (custom level 3 for the Evo Plus).
2. Add 1 tbsp olive oil and ½ cup/30g panko breadcrumbs to the pot, stir regularly until golden brown. Press cancel and pour into a bowl. Mix in ¼ tsp salt, ¼ tsp freshly ground black pepper and ¼ tsp cayenne pepper. Set aside for later.
3. Clean the inner pot.
4. Pour 1 cup of water (for pressure) into the pot, with your trivet. Place the cauliflower florets in a steamer basket or directly on the trivet.
5. Place the lid on the Instant Pot, set valve to seal, select manual high pressure (pressure cook custom high on Evo Plus) for 1 minute.
6. When Instant Pot beeps, quick release the pressure.
7. When pin drops, open the lid. Press cancel.
8. Reserve the cauliflower, empty the water, dry the pot, and return to the Instant Pot.
9. Select sauté mode as above. Add 3 ½ tbsp unsalted butter and allow to melt.
10. Sieve 1/3 cup all-purpose/plain flour into the pot, stir continuously (1 to 2) minutes until you have a thick foamy paste just starting to turn golden.
11. Gradually, stir in 2 cups/500 ml of milk, a little at a time making sure that the milk has absorbed completely each time before adding more. Once all the milk has been added, whisk continuously until you have a thin white sauce.
12. Add 1 tsp of your favourite mustard, ¼ tsp salt, ¼ tsp freshly ground black pepper and stir in 1 cup/100g of grated cheddar.
13. Add the reserved cauliflower back into the pot and allow to warm through. Press cancel.
14. Pour into a serving dish, sprinkle over reserved panko and serve.

- 2 medium tomatoes (chopped into eighths)
- ½ tsp chilli pickle
- ½ tsp mango chutney
- 1 tsp garam masala
- Handful fresh cilantro/coriander leaves

PREPARATION STEPS

1. Add 2 cups/500 ml of water, ½ tsp turmeric, ½ tsp salt, and 3 cups/300g of new potatoes (peeled and cut into bite size pieces) to the pot.
2. Place the lid on the Instant Pot, set valve to seal, select manual high pressure (pressure cook custom high on Evo Plus) for 10 minutes.
3. When Instant Pot beeps, quick release pressure.
4. When pin drops, open the lid. Press cancel.
5. Drain the potatoes and reserve for later.
6. Press the sauté button on the Instant Pot on normal heat, (custom level 3 for the Evo Plus).
7. Once display says HOT, add 3 tbsp vegetable oil or ghee, 1 tsp mustard seeds, ½ tsp fennel seeds, and ½ tsp cumin seeds.
8. When mustard seeds start to pop, add 1 medium onion (finely chopped), and ½ tsp salt. Sauté until translucent, stirring occasionally.
9. Add 3 garlic cloves (peeled and finely chopped), 1 red chilli (finely sliced), and a handful of fresh cilantro/coriander stalks, cook for 2 minutes, stirring occasionally.
10. Pour in a little hot water if needed, to prevent burning.
11. Add 2 medium tomatoes (chopped into eighths), and reserved potatoes. Cook for 2 minutes, stirring occasionally.
12. Stir in ½ tsp chilli pickle, ½ tsp mango chutney, 1 tsp garam masala and half of the reserved cilantro/coriander leaves.
13. Add a little hot water if a sauce is preferred.
14. Stir and leave for a minute. Press cancel.
15. Serve garnished with remaining cilantro/coriander leaves.

Bombay Potatoes

One of the most popular Indian side dishes.

SERVES 2

INGREDIENTS

- 2 cups/500 ml of water
- ½ tsp turmeric
- ½ tsp salt
- 3 cups/300g new potatoes (peeled and cut into bite size pieces)
- 3 tbsp vegetable oil or ghee
- 1 tsp mustard seeds
- ½ tsp fennel seeds
- ½ tsp cumin seeds
- 1 medium onion (finely chopped)
- ½ tsp salt
- 3 garlic cloves (peeled and finely chopped)
- 1 red chilli (finely sliced)
- Handful fresh cilantro/coriander stalks

Homemade Baked Beans

As tasty as canned - without the artificial additives.

SERVES 10

INGREDIENTS

- 1 lb/450g dried navy/haricot beans
- 8 cups/2 ltrs water
- 1 tbsp olive oil
- 2 tsp salt
- 2 cups/500 ml vegetable or chicken stock
- 1 cup water
- 2 tsp Worcestershire sauce
- 6 tbsp tomato ketchup
- 2 tbsp tomato puree/paste
- 3 tbsp brown sugar
- 1 tbsp apple cider vinegar
- ½ tsp garlic powder
- ½ tsp onion powder
- ½ tsp freshly ground black pepper
- 1 tsp salt
- 3 tbsp cornstarch/cornflour
- 3 tbsp cold water

PREPARATION STEPS

1. 1 lb/450g dried navy/haricot beans, 8 cups/2 ltrs of water, 1 tbsp olive oil and 2 tsp salt to the pot. (Do not fill the pot more than half full).

2. Place lid on Instant Pot, set valve to seal, select manual high pressure (pressure cook custom high on Evo Plus) 30 minutes.

3. When Instant Pot beeps press cancel, allow natural release of the pressure until pressure valve release pin drops (20 to 30 minutes).

4. Strain the beans, discard the liquid, and set aside.

5. Clean inner pot. Add 2 tsp salt, 2 cups/500 ml vegetable or chicken stock, 1 cup water, 2 tsp Worcestershire sauce, 6 tbsp tomato ketchup, 2 tbsp tomato puree/paste, 3 tbsp brown sugar, 1 tbsp apple cider vinegar, ½ tsp garlic powder, ½ tsp onion powder and ½ tsp freshly ground black pepper.

6. Stir, then add reserved beans.

7. Press the sauté button on the Instant Pot on normal heat, (custom level 3 for the Evo Plus). Bring to a simmer, then reduce the heat on the Instant Pot to low, (custom level 1 for the Evo Plus). Simmer for 20 minutes without a lid, stirring occasionally so that the beans don't catch the bottom of the pot.

8. Mix 3 tbsp cornstarch/cornflour with 3 tbsp cold water, stir into the pot and cook for 2 minutes to thicken.

9. Check for seasoning and serve, traditionally served on hot buttered toast.

INGREDIENTS

- 2 cups/260g bread flour
- 1 tsp salt
- ½ tsp instant yeast
- 1 cup/285g plain Greek yogurt (freshly made or opened)

PREPARATION STEPS

1. In a bowl, mix 2 cups/260g bread flour, 1 tsp salt, and ½ tsp instant yeast.

2. Add 1 cup/285g of plain Greek yogurt and mix until you have a dough, add more yogurt if needed form into a fairly wet dough (mix for 5-6 minutes).

3. Line the inner pot with baking parchment and place the dough inside.

4. Place the lid on, don't set to seal, (remove rubber seal if tainted to avoid onion flavored bread).

5. On your Instant Pot, select yogurt.

6. Make sure your Instant Pot is set to normal 4 hours. Press adjust until display shows 4.00. Display will go to 0.00 and count up.

7. On Duo Evo Plus select yogurt/custom/4.00/temp 110°/f/43°/c/start. Display will count down once up to temp.

8. After proving for 4 hours, remove the dough from the pot, place on a floured surface. Gently shape into a ball, cover with little extra flour and a dish towel.

9. In the meantime, place a Dutch oven into your oven, pre heat to 450°/f / 230°/c for 30 minutes.

10. After 30 minutes place the dough into the Dutch oven. Flour then score the top and place the lid on.

11. Bake for 25 minutes, then remove lid and bake for another 10 minutes or until browned.

12. Switch off the oven leaving the door ajar for 30 minutes, then remove from Dutch oven and cool on a wire rack.

    Tip: It's a good idea to place your Dutch oven on a metal baking tray, this prevents the bottom of the bread from burning.

Instant Pot Bread

Delicious easy to make bread.

SERVES 6

PREPARATION STEPS

1. Fill inner pot to ¾ full with hot water. Select sous vide mode custom 85 °/c/185 °/f, set time to 30 minutes and bring up to temperature.

2. In a small bowl, mix 1 tbsp Sriracha chilli sauce, 1 tsp powder/icing sugar and 1 tbsp unsalted butter, add to a sous vide compatible zipper type bag, along with the 2 ears of corn.

3. Remove as much of the air as you can by lowering the bag into a bowl of water, using the water to push the air out of the bag, being careful not to allow any water into the bag. Seal while immersed or use a vacuum sealer.

4. Once up to temperature, cook for 30 minutes.

5. When cooked, remove from water bath, open bag, and pour out. Season with freshly ground black pepper and chilli flakes to taste.

Sous Vide Chilli Butter Corn

Succulent, perfectly cooked corn- packed with flavour.

SERVES 2

INGREDIENTS

- 2 ears of corn
- 1 tbsp Sriracha chilli sauce
- 1 tsp powder/icing sugar
- 1 tbsp unsalted butter
- Freshly ground black pepper and chilli flakes to taste

PREPARATION STEPS

1. Add 2 cups/200g macaroni, ½ tsp salt and 1 ½ cups/375 ml cold water (enough to just cover pasta).

2. Place lid on Instant Pot, set valve to seal, select manual high pressure (pressure cook custom high on Evo Plus) 2 minutes.

3. When Instant Pot beeps allow 5 minutes natural pressure release, then open the valve to release the rest of the pressure. Press cancel. Drain off any excess water then stir 1 tbsp of the unsalted butter into the macaroni. Pour into an oven proof dish.

4. In a small bowl, mix ½ cup/30g panko breadcrumbs with 1 ½ tbsp of the unsalted butter (melted), add a pinch of salt then reserve.

5. Pre heat your oven to 350°/f/180 °/c.

6. Press the sauté button on the Instant Pot on less heat, (custom level 1 for the Evo Plus).

7. Melt 2 ½ tbsp of the unsalted butter, add ¼ cup/65g of all-purpose/plain flour. Stir constantly for 1 minute.

8. Add 2 cup/480 ml of milk a little at a time, mix to incorporate the paste into the milk, mix until lump free using a whisk.

9. Cook, stirring constantly for 5 to 8 minutes until thickened to a creamy consistency. Press cancel.

10. Stir in 1 cup/100g of grated cheddar and ½ cup/50g of grated mozzarella (cheese does not need to melt). Add salt and freshly ground black pepper until perfectly seasoned.

11. Pour the sauce over the macaroni in the oven proof dish. Stir and sprinkle on breadcrumb topping.

12. Bake for 20 minutes, or until topping is golden.

Jenny's Baked Mac & Cheese

Simple, tasty, and crunchy.

SERVES 4

INGREDIENTS

- 2 cups/200g macaroni
- ½ tsp salt (to taste)
- 1 ½ cups/375 ml cold water (enough to just cover pasta)
- 5 tbsp unsalted butter
- ½ cup/30g panko breadcrumbs
- ¼ cup/65g all-purpose/plain flour
- 2 cups/480 ml milk
- 1 cup/100g grated cheddar
- ½ cup/50g grated mozzarella
- Freshly ground black pepper (to taste)

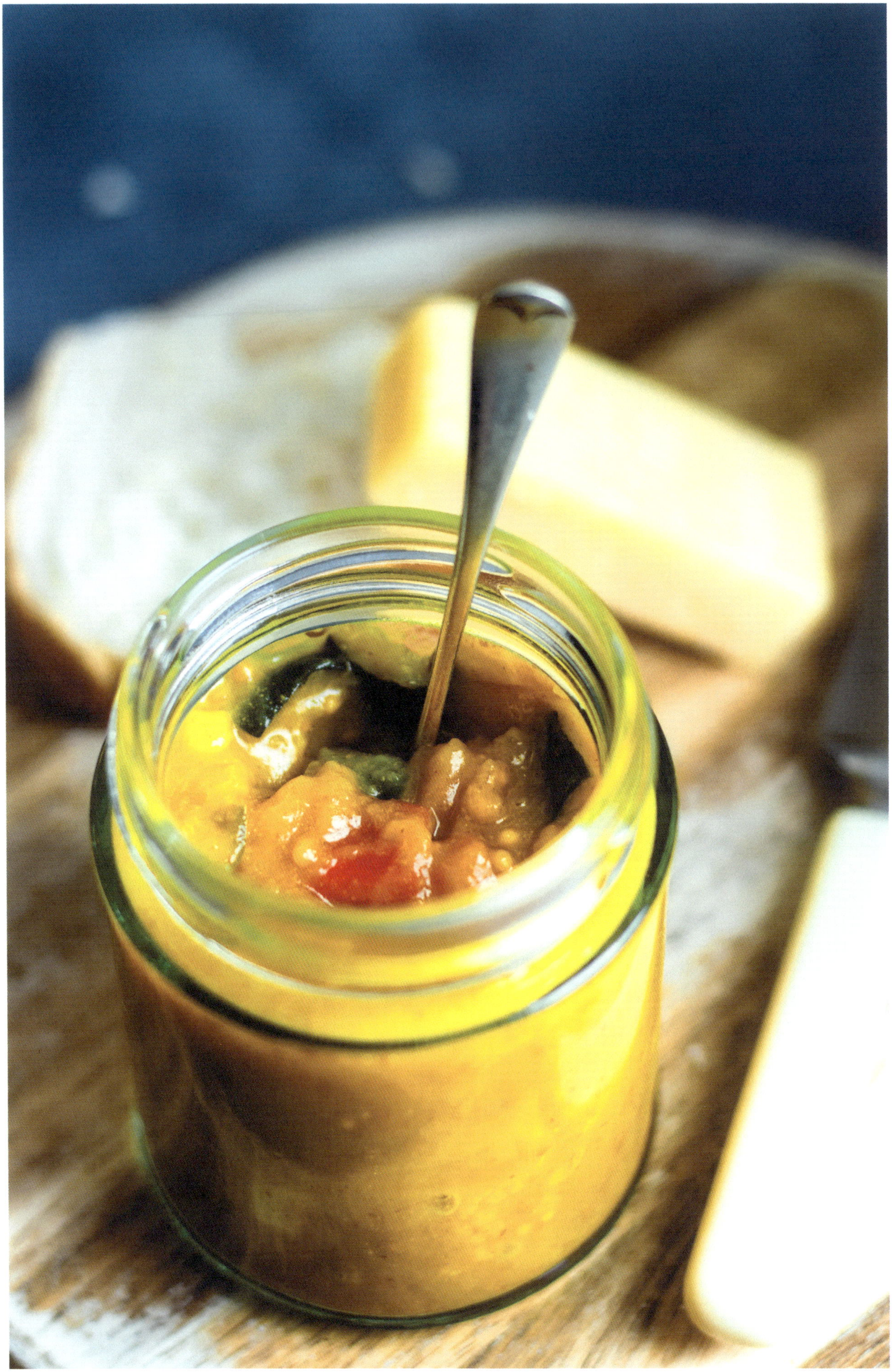

Condiments etc

Quark

An easy to make, low fat substitute for cream.

INGREDIENTS

- 4 cups/1 ltr cultured buttermilk

PREPARATION STEPS

1. Pour 4 cups/1 ltr cultured buttermilk into the pot (time and temperature remain the same for different amounts).
2. On your Instant Pot select yogurt.
3. Make sure your Instant Pot is set to normal 8 hours, press adjust until display shows 8.00. Display will go to 0.00 and count up.
4. On Duo Evo Plus select yogurt/custom/8.00/temp 110°/f/43°/c/start. Display will count down once up to temp.
5. After 8 hours, once the Instant Pot has beeped, remove lid.
6. Place a cheesecloth over a colander, place the colander over a large bowl.
7. Pour the quark into the colander and leave at room temperature for 5 hours, whilst the whey drains.
8. Store sealed in the refrigerator for up to 10 days, or for up to 3 months in the freezer.

PREPARATION STEPS

1. Place a small plate in your freezer, for a jam set test.
2. 1 ¾ cups/350g fresh or frozen cherries (pitted and rinsed), 1 ¾ cups/350g jam sugar and the juice of 1 lemon to the inner pot, give it a stir to combine.
3. Place lid on Instant Pot, set valve to seal, select manual high pressure (pressure cook custom high on Evo Plus) for 2 minutes.
4. When Instant Pot beeps, allow 15 minutes natural pressure release.
5. In the meantime, wash an empty jar well, pouring boiling water into and over it, not forgetting the lid.
6. After 15 minutes, open valve to release any remaining pressure. Press cancel and remove lid.
7. Press the sauté button on the Instant Pot on normal heat, (custom level 3 for the Evo Plus).
8. Reduce the jam for 5 minutes, stirring occasionally. Spoon a little of the jam onto the small plate from the freezer, leave for a few seconds. Gently push the jam with the spoon, if you can see a skin and it wrinkles the jam is ready, if not, place the small plate back in the freezer and carry on reducing for further 3 minutes, then test again, repeat until it wrinkles.
9. Press cancel and remove inner pot. Carefully drain the hot water from the jar.
10. Stir 1 tsp almond extract into the jam, then carefully pour the jam into the jar.
11. Place the lid on and turn the jar upside down. Leave for five minutes on a towel before turning the right way up, this helps to seal the jar.
12. Store in the fridge for up to six weeks.
13. Can be frozen for up to six months. Make sure to leave at least ½ inch/1.5 cm space at the top of the jar for the jam to expand.

Dark Cherry Almond Jam

An amazing cherry jam with a beautiful almond flavor.

INGREDIENTS

- 1 ¾ cups/350g fresh or frozen cherries (pitted and rinsed)
- 1 ¾ cups/350g jam sugar
- Juice of 1 lemon
- 1 tsp almond extract

Chicken Stock

A stock can make or break a good dish. A simple thing to make in the Instant Pot.

INGREDIENTS

- 1 leftover chicken carcass
- 2 cups/500 ml of cold water
- 1 onion (quartered)
- 1 carrot (roughly chopped)
- 2 celery stalks (roughly chopped)
- 2 garlic cloves

PREPARATION STEPS

1. Break down 1 leftover chicken carcass with a pair of kitchen scissors, placing into the pot along with the rest of the ingredients.

2. Place lid on Instant Pot, set valve to seal, select manual high pressure (pressure cook custom high on Evo Plus) for one hour.

3. When Instant Pot beeps, allow 10 minutes natural pressure release, then open the valve to release the rest of the pressure.

4. When pin drops, open the lid.

5. Strain the stock into a jug and cool to room temperature in ice water then refrigerate.

6. Once cool, check for thin layer of solid fat on the surface and remove.

7. Cover and refrigerate, use within three days.

8. Suitable for freezing.

PREPARATION STEPS

1. Place 3 ½ oz/100g white bread (crusts removed) in a food processor, pulse to make breadcrumbs and set aside.

2. Press the sauté button on the Instant Pot on normal heat, (custom level 3 for the Evo Plus).

3. Once display says HOT, add 1 medium onion (peeled and cut into eighths), 2 cloves, 3 black peppercorns, 1 bay leaf, 1 pinch ground mace, 1 pinch ground nutmeg and 1 ¼ cups/300 ml milk.

4. Cook for 4 minutes stirring regularly. Press cancel.

5. Remove inner pot, cover, and set aside for 1 hour for flavors to infuse, pour through a sieve into a jug, discarding the solids and transferring the milk back into the Instant Pot.

6. Select sous vide mode custom 60 °/c/140 °/f, set minimum time and bring up to temperature.

7. Once up to temperature, add infused milk and reserved breadcrumbs.

8. Place the lid on with the vent open, cook for 15 minutes stirring occasionally. Press cancel.

9. Stir in 2 tbsp unsalted butter, ¼ tsp salt and 1 pinch freshly ground black pepper.

10. Serve hot, traditionally with roasted poultry.

Bread Sauce

A traditional British Christmas classic.

SERVES 4

INGREDIENTS

- 3 ½ oz/100g white bread (crusts removed)
- 1 medium onion (peeled and cut into eighths)
- 2 cloves
- 3 black peppercorns
- 1 bay leaf
- 1 pinch ground mace
- 1 pinch ground nutmeg
- 1 ¼ cups/300 ml milk
- 2 tbsp unsalted butter
- ¼ tsp salt
- 1 pinch freshly ground black pepper

Mango Chutney

Sweet & tangy, poppadums are lost without it.

MAKES APPROX 16 US FL OZ / 2 CUPS / 500 ML

INGREDIENTS

- 2 tbsp olive oil
- 8 cardamom pods (crushed)
- 6 cloves
- ½ tsp nigella seeds
- ½ tsp cumin seeds
- ¼ tsp fenugreek seeds
- 1 inch/3 cm fresh ginger (grated)
- 2 garlic cloves (crushed)
- 1 red chilli (finely chopped)
- 1 1/3 cups/300 ml cider vinegar
- 1 ¼ cups/250g sugar
- 3 large ripe mangoes (peeled and diced)
- ¼ tsp turmeric powder
- ¼ tsp freshly ground black pepper
- 1 tsp salt

PREPARATION STEPS

1. Select the sauté button on the Instant Pot on normal heat, (custom level 3 for the Evo Plus) once display says HOT, add 2 tbsp of olive oil.
2. Add the 8 cardamom pods (crushed), 6 cloves, ½ tsp nigella seeds, ½ tsp cumin seeds and ¼ tsp fenugreek seeds. Stir for 1 minute.
3. Add 1 inch/3 cm fresh ginger (grated), 2 garlic cloves (crushed), 1 red chilli (finely chopped).
4. Stir regularly for 1 minute.
5. Stir in, 1 1/3 cups/300 ml cider vinegar, 1 ¼ cups/250g sugar, 3 large ripe mangoes (peeled and diced), ¼ tsp turmeric powder, ¼ tsp freshly ground black pepper and 1 tsp salt. Press cancel.
6. Place lid on Instant Pot, set valve to seal, select manual low pressure (pressure cook custom low on Evo Plus) for 10 minutes.
7. When Instant Pot beeps, quick release pressure. Press cancel.
8. Divide among sterilised jars, seal, and keep refrigerated for up to six months.

Piccalilli

So much better than the bought version.

MAKES APPROX 16 US FL OZ / 2 CUPs / 500 ML

INGREDIENTS

- 1 lb/450g mixed vegetables cut into bite sized pieces, (cauliflower, green beans, shallots, pearl onions, cucumber deseeded, courgettes deseeded, peppers, carrots, chilli's, and garlic)
- 2 tbsp + 1 tsp salt
- 2 tbsp olive oil
- 1 tbsp yellow mustard seeds
- 1 tbsp ground coriander
- 1 tbsp ground turmeric
- 1 tbsp English mustard powder
- 1 ¼ cups/300 ml + ¼ cup/60 ml cider vinegar
- ½ cup/100g granulated sugar
- 2 tbsp cornstarch/cornflour

PREPARATION STEPS

1. Place 1 lb/450g mixed vegetables in a colander over a bowl, sprinkle over 2 tbsp salt and mix well. Cover and leave in a cool place overnight.
2. The following day, rinse vegetables in cold water, drain thoroughly then dry with kitchen towel.
3. Press the sauté button on the Instant Pot on normal heat, (custom level 3 for the Evo Plus).
4. Once display says HOT, add 2 tbsp olive oil and 1 tbsp yellow mustard seeds. Sauté until seeds start to pop. Add 1 tbsp ground coriander and 1 tbsp ground turmeric, stir for 10 seconds then add 1 tbsp English mustard powder. Slowly stir in 1 ¼ cups/300 ml of cider vinegar, 1 tsp salt and ½ cup/100g granulated sugar. Stir, bring to the boil, reduce for 10 minutes stirring regularly. Press cancel.
5. Add drained vegetables and stir until coated in the sauce.
6. Place the lid on the Instant Pot, set valve to seal, select manual high pressure (pressure cook custom high on Evo Plus) for 0 minutes.
7. When Instant Pot beeps, quick release the pressure.
8. When pin drops, open the lid. Press cancel.
9. Select sauté as above, mix together ¼ cup/60 ml cider vinegar and 2 tbsp cornstarch /cornflour, add to the pot. Stir gently to thicken.
10. Pour into hot sterilized jars and seal immediately. Leave for at least 4 weeks for flavors to develop before using, ensuring a good sale by checking that the lid is depressed at the centre.
11. Store at room temperature, unopened for up to 12 months. Once opened refrigerate and use within 2 weeks.

Sous Vide Thyme Infused Oil

A simple method to extract the maximum flavour into your infused oils.

MAKES APPROX 8 US FL OZ / 1 CUP / 250 ML

INGREDIENTS

- 1 cup/250 ml olive oil
- ½ oz/15g fresh thyme (see tip)

PREPARATION STEPS

1. Fill inner pot to ¾ full with hot water. Select sous vide mode custom 55 °/c/131 °/f, set time for 3 hours and bring up to temperature.
2. Combine 1 cup/250 ml of olive oil and ½ oz/15g. fresh thyme in a sous vide compatible zipper type bag.
3. Remove as much of the air as you can by lowering the bag into a bowl of water, using the water to push the air out of the bag, being careful not to allow any water into the bag. Seal while immersed or use a vacuum sealer.
4. Once up to temperature cook for 3 hours.
5. After 3 hours, place in an ice bath to chill, then strain into a clean jar.
6. Keep refrigerated for up to 2 weeks.
7. Drizzle over roasted vegetables, grilled meats, or seafood.

Tip: If you want to give your oil a hint of smoke, try grilling your thyme on the barbecue for a few minutes beforehand.

PREPARATION STEPS

1. Fill inner pot to ½ full with hot water. Select sous vide mode custom 60 °/c/140 °/f, set time for 2 hours and bring up to temperature.

2. Add 1 cup/250 ml of water to a jug, 1 cup/250 ml white of wine vinegar, ¼ cup/60g sugar and 2 tsp salt, mix until sugar and salt are dissolved.

3. Slice 2 small cucumbers (sliced 0.2 inch/0.5 cm), 0.6 oz/18g of fresh dill (finely chopped), 2 fresh red chillies (sliced) or use dried chilli flakes (to taste), ½ a medium red onion (sliced 0.2 inch/0.5 cm) and 2 tsp pickling spice. Stir well.

4. Layer ingredients into sterilized jars, don't worry too much about getting the amounts wrong, it's not critical.

5. Pack in as much as you can, then add the solution filling up to the neck of the jar. Remove any air by pushing the contents down and gently tapping the jar on the counter, then top up to 0.4 inch/1 cm from the top of the jar.

6. Tighten the lid finger tight.

7. Once up to temperature, fully submerge the jars in the water bath and leave for 2 hours. Press cancel.

8. After two hours take out of the water bath and leave to cool to room temperature for about 1 ½ hours, refrigerate overnight.

9. If the centre of the lid is depressed the seal is good. You can store at room temperature unopened for up to six months. Once opened, refrigerate, and use within 2 weeks.

Tip: Using this water, vinegar, sugar, salt ratio at 60 °/c/140 °/f, you can pretty much pickle whatever you like.

Sous Vide Pickles

Low temperature pickling gives an extra crunch.

MAKES APPROX 32 US FL OZ / 4 CUPs / 1 LTR

INGREDIENTS

- 1 cup/250 ml water
- 1 cup/250 ml white wine vinegar
- ¼ cup/60g sugar
- 2 tsp salt
- 2 small cucumbers (sliced 0.2 inch/ 0.5 cm)
- 0.6 oz/18g fresh dill (finely chopped)
- 2 fresh red chillies (sliced) or dried chilli flakes (to taste)
- ½ medium red onion (sliced 0.2 inch/ 0.5 cm)
- 2 tsp pickling spice

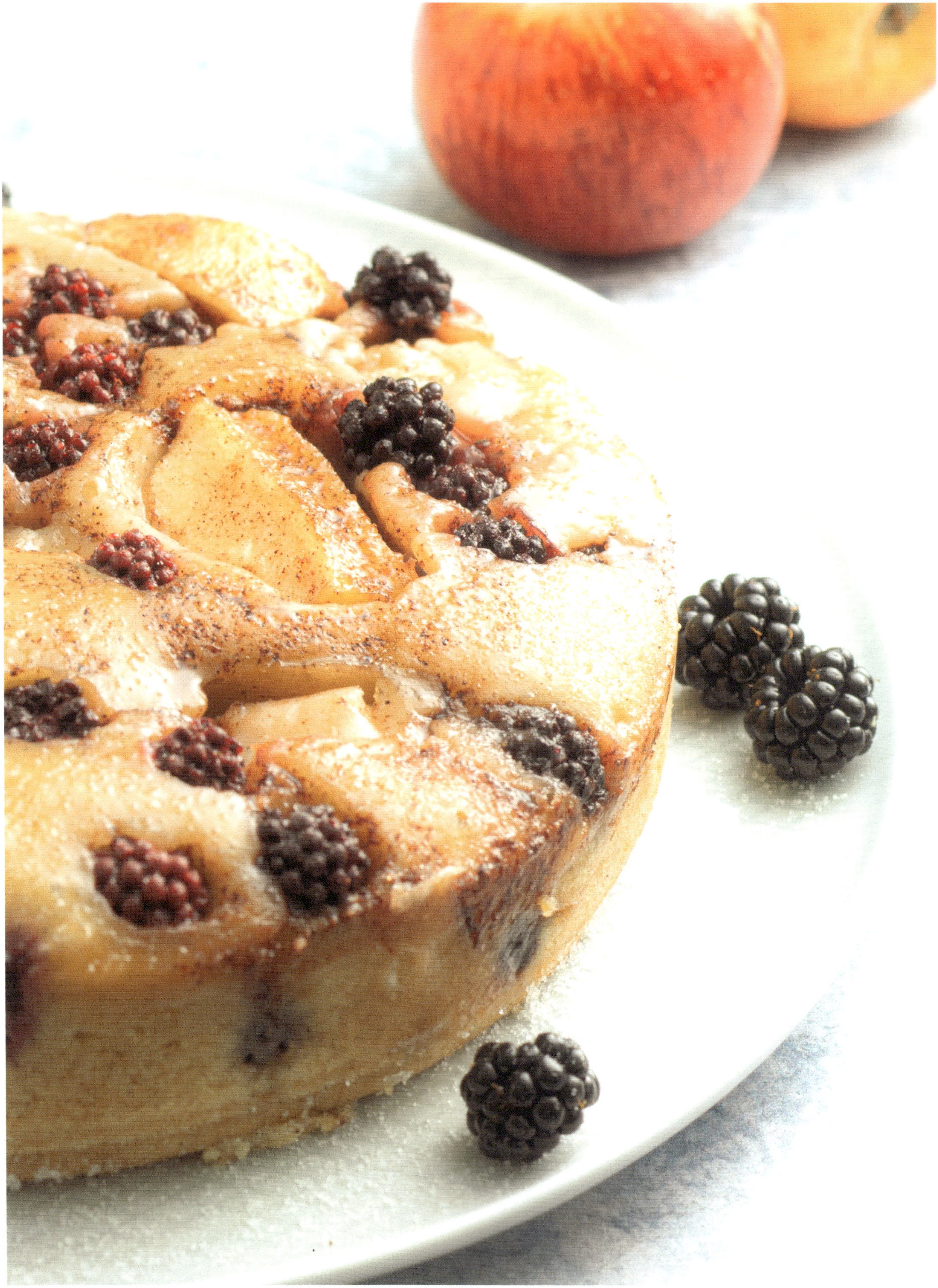

Sweets & Desserts

Baked Granola Apples

Forgot to make dessert? Grab some apples…

SERVES 4

INGREDIENTS

- 4 large apples
- 4 tbsp salted butter (room temperature)
- ¼ cup/60g maple syrup
- ¾ cup/75g granola
- 1 tsp all spice

PREPARATION STEPS

1. Core 4 large apples.
2. In a bowl, mix 4 tbsp salted butter (room temperature), ¼ cup/60g maple syrup, ¾ cup/75g granola and 1 tsp all spice.
3. Cut 4 pieces of foil big enough to wrap the apples.
4. Place each apple on a piece of foil.
5. Fill the cored apples with the mixture and wrap in the foil.
6. Place your trivet into the Instant Pot, pour in 1 cup of cold water into the inner pot.
7. Place the wrapped apples on the trivet.
8. Place lid on Instant Pot, set valve to seal, select manual high pressure (pressure cook custom high on Evo Plus) for 20 minutes.
9. When Instant Pot beeps, quick release pressure. Press cancel.
10. Serve apples on their own, with custard, cream, or ice cream.

PREPARATION STEPS

1. Place trivet into the Instant Pot, pour 1 ½ cups/375 ml of cold water into the inner pot.

2. In an oven safe ceramic bowl, mix 1 ½ cups/375 ml of your preferred milk, ½ cup/100g arborio rice/risotto/pudding rice (unwashed), 1 tbsp sugar, 1/8 tsp salt and 1/8 tsp of ground nutmeg.

3. Place oven safe bowl on trivet and lower into instant pot.

4. Place lid on Instant Pot, set valve to seal, select manual high pressure (pressure cook custom high on Evo Plus) for 40 minutes.

5. When Instant Pot beeps, quick release pressure.

6. Serve immediately. If saving, chill storing in refrigerator for up to 3 days.

Traditional Rice Pudding

Pot in pot method allows you the freedom to use any milk, without the risk of burning or sticking.

SERVES 4

INGREDIENTS

POT IN POT METHOD

- 1 ½ cups/375 ml of cold water (for pressure)
- 1 ½ cups/375 ml of your preferred milk
- ½ cup/100g arborio rice/risotto/pudding rice (unwashed)
- 1 tbsp sugar
- 1/8 tsp salt
- 1/8 tsp ground nutmeg

Aromatic Rice Pudding

A Chai influenced dessert.

Fragrant spices complimented with lime zest.

SERVES 4

INGREDIENTS

POT IN POT METHOD

- 1 ½ cups/375 ml of cold water in pot (for pressure)
- 1 vanilla pod
- 1 cardamom pod
- 2 cloves
- 1 cinnamon stick (3 inch/7.5 cm. ½ cup/100g arborio/risotto/pudding rice (unwashed)
- 1 x 14 oz/400g can of coconut milk or preferred milk
- 1 tbsp sugar
- ¼ tsp salt
- Zest of 1 lime

PREPARATION STEPS

1. Press the sauté button on the Instant Pot on normal heat, (custom level 3 for the Evo Plus) once display says HOT, add 1 vanilla pod, 1 cardamom pod, 2 cloves and 1 cinnamon stick (3 inch/7.5 cm).

2. Toast for around 30 seconds to release aroma. Press cancel and empty spices into a ceramic oven safe bowl.

3. Take out the vanilla pod, flatten with the edge of a knife and cut the vanilla bean in half lengthways and scrape out seeds. Add vanilla seeds and pod back to the bowl with the rest of the spices.

4. Pour 1 ½ cups/375 ml of cold water into the inner pot.

5. In the oven safe ceramic bowl, mix ½ cup/100g of arborio rice/risotto/pudding rice, 1 x 14 oz/400g can of coconut milk or preferred milk, 1 tbsp sugar, ¼ tsp salt and zest of half of the lime, save the other half to serve.

6. Place oven safe ceramic bowl on trivet and lower into Instant Pot.

7. Place lid on Instant Pot, set valve to seal, select manual high pressure (pressure cook custom high on Evo Plus) for 40 minutes.

8. When Instant Pot beeps, quick release pressure. Press cancel.

9. Sprinkle with reserved lime zest and serve immediately.

10. Once cool store in refrigerator for up to 3 days.

Tip: If saving, remove spices.

PREPARATION STEPS

1. Pour 2 cups/300g of defrosted ice cream into a large mixing bowl and stir until smooth.
2. In a separate bowl mix 1 cup/110g of self-rising flour, ¼ cup/50g of caster sugar and ¼ tsp of salt, add to the ice cream.
3. Stir with a spatula, avoid over mixing (don't worry a few small lumps).
4. Pour the mix into a 6.5 inch/16.5 cm greased loaf pan (the Instant Pot silicone loaf pan is ideal).
5. Pour 1 cup/250 ml of water into the Instant Pot, place a trivet into the pot and place the loaf pan on top of the trivet.
6. Place lid on Instant Pot, set valve to seal, select manual high pressure (pressure cook custom high on Evo Plus) for 35 minutes.
7. When Instant Pot beeps, press cancel. Allow 5 minutes natural pressure release, then open the valve to release the rest of the pressure.
8. When pin drops, take out the loaf pan and let it cool for 10 to 15 minutes, then remove the loaf onto a plate.
9. Slice and serve with butter or ice cream.

Ice Cream Bread

Amazing ice cream bread. Choose a flavour!

SERVES 4

INGREDIENTS

- 2 cups/300g full fat ice cream (defrosted in refrigerator overnight)
- 1 cup/110g self-rising flour
- ¼ cup/50g caster sugar
- ¼ tsp of salt
- Butter or cooking spray for greasing loaf pan
- 1 cup/250 ml of water for pressure

Poached Pears in Cranberry Juice

Traditionally poached in wine, cranberry juice can be used instead as a non-alcoholic but no less delicious alternative.

SERVES 4

INGREDIENTS

- 1 ¼ cups/300 ml unsweetened cranberry juice
- 6 tbsp light brown sugar
- 1 cinnamon stick
- 4 cloves
- 4 ripe pears (peeled, bottoms sliced off)

PREPARATION STEPS

1. Press the sauté button on the Instant Pot on normal heat, (custom level 3 for the Evo Plus).
2. Add the 1 ¼ cups/300 ml of cranberry juice, 6 tbsp light brown sugar, 1 cinnamon stick and 4 cloves.
3. Heat until the sugar has melted, and the sauce has reduced a little.
4. Add 4 ripe pears (peeled, bottoms sliced off) to the pot.
5. Place lid on, set valve to seal, select manual high pressure (pressure cook custom high on Evo Plus) for 10 minutes.
6. When Instant Pot beeps, press cancel. Quick release pressure.
7. Perfect served with homemade yogurt.

INGREDIENTS

POT IN POT METHOD

- 1 cup/250 ml of cold water in pot for pressure
- 4 slices of white bread (stale bread is traditionally used)
- 1 oz/30g unsalted butter
- ½ cup/80g sultanas or raisins
- 2 tsp ground cinnamon
- 2 large eggs
- 2 tbsp light brown sugar
- 1 ¾ cups/400 ml preferred milk
- 1 tsp vanilla extract

PREPARATION STEPS

1. Place trivet into the Instant Pot, pour 1 cup/250 ml of cold water into the inner pot.

2. Spread 1 oz/30g unsalted butter on both sides of the 4 slices of bread, then tear into small chunks.

3. Add half the bread, to the oven safe ceramic bowl, followed by half the sultanas or raisins and half the ground cinnamon. Repeat this step for a second layer.

4. In a bowl, whisk the 2 large eggs, and 2 tbsp light brown sugar, whisk in 1 ¾ cups/400 ml of preferred milk and 1 tsp vanilla extract.

5. Pour the milk mixture over the bread.

6. Place oven safe ceramic bowl on trivet and lower into instant pot.

7. Place lid on Instant Pot, set valve to seal, select manual high pressure (pressure cook custom high on Evo Plus) for 20 minutes.

8. When Instant Pot beeps, press cancel. Quick release pressure.

9. Serve with custard, cream, or ice cream.

Tip: Tastes best if you let it cool for 10-15 minutes.

Bread & Butter Pudding

An age old British staple.

SERVES 6

Toasted Sweet Coconut Popcorn

Easy, fun to make, and delicious.

SERVES 4

INGREDIENTS

- 2 tbsp extra virgin coconut oil
- 1/3 cup/80g (new unopened pack) popcorn kernels
- 1 cup/100g desiccated coconut
- ½ cup/100g salted butter
- ¼ cup/50g sugar
- ¼ tsp coconut extract

PREPARATION STEPS

1. Press the sauté button on the Instant Pot on more (press adjust until led indicates more), (custom level 6 for the Evo Plus).

2. Once display says HOT, melt 2 tbsp extra virgin coconut oil. Once shimmering, add 1/3 cup/80g (new unopened pack) popcorn kernels.

3. Stir with a spatula, spreading the kernels across the bottom of the pot for about 1 minute.

4. Place a lid or plate on the Instant Pot (the Instant Pot glass lid is ideal for this).

5. After about 2 minutes the corn will start popping, let it pop for about 5 minutes. When popping slows down to one pop every 15 seconds shake the pot, let any uncooked kernels pop. Press cancel.

6. Remove the inner pot from the Instant Pot and pour the popcorn into a bowl.

7. Pour 1 cup/100g desiccated coconut onto a large baking sheet, even out and bake in a pre-heated oven at 200 °/c/400 °/f for 2 minutes or until lightly toasted.

8. Remove from the oven and set to one side.

9. Press the sauté button on the Instant Pot on normal heat, (custom level 3 for the Evo Plus).

10. Once display says HOT, melt ½ cup/100g salted butter, then add ¼ cup/50g sugar, stir to dissolve.

11. Bring to a boil, let boil for 1 to 2 minutes. Press cancel, remove inner pot, and add ¼ tsp coconut extract.

12. Add reserved toasted coconut and combine. Pour over the popcorn to coat.

PREPARATION STEPS

1. In a bowl mix 1 ¼ cups/130g of self-rising flour, ¼ tsp of salt and ½ cup/60g of suet together with enough of the ½ cup/125 ml of water to make a firm dough.
2. Roll out the dough on a lightly floured surface to make a 6 inch/15 cm square.
3. Spread with ½ cup/150g of marmalade and roll up, sprinkle all over with caster sugar.
4. Loosely wrap in cling film and then in foil.
5. Place the trivet into the inner pot and add 1 cup/ 250 ml of water to the pot.
6. Place lid on, set valve to seal, select manual high pressure (pressure cook custom high on Evo Plus) for 40 minutes.
7. When Instant Pot beeps, press cancel. Quick release the pressure.
8. Slice the roly-poly into generous pieces, serving with a generous helping of warm custard.

Tip: This recipe works great with almost any jam / sweet preserve you have.

Marmalade Roly-Poly

Old fashioned comfort food.

SERVES 4

INGREDIENTS

- 1 ¼ cup/130g self-rising flour
- ¼ tsp salt
- ½ cup/60g suet
- ½ cup/125 ml water
- ½ cup/150g thick marmalade
- Good sprinkle of caster sugar
- 1 cup/250 ml water for pressure

Autumn Cake

A beautifully moist cake loaded with Autumnal fruit.

SERVES 8

INGREDIENTS

- 1 cup/250 ml of cold water (for pressure)
- 1 ½ cups/150g apples (cored, peeled and diced)
- 1 cup/150g fresh blackberries
- ½ tbsp ground cinnamon
- 2 tbsp granulated sugar
- 1 ½ cups/150g all-purpose/plain flour
- ½ tbsp baking powder
- ½ tsp salt
- ½ cup/125 ml vegetable oil
- ¾ cup/130g light brown sugar
- 2 tbsp water
- 1 ½ tsp vanilla extract
- 2 large eggs (room temperature)
- Butter for greasing
- Caster sugar for decoration

PREPARATION STEPS

1. Combine 1 ½ cups/150g apples (cored, peeled and diced), 1 cup/150g fresh blackberries, ½ tbsp ground cinnamon and 2 tbsp granulated sugar. Set aside.
2. In a large bowl mix dry ingredients, 1 ½ cups/150g all-purpose/plain flour, ½ tbsp baking powder and ½ tsp salt. Set aside.
3. In a separate bowl whisk wet ingredients, ½ cup/125 ml vegetable oil, ¾ cup/130g light brown sugar, 2 tbsp water, 1 ½ tsp vanilla extract and 2 large eggs (room temperature).
4. Mix wet and dry ingredients together to form a thick batter.
5. Grease a 7 inch/17.5 cm round (springform ideally) cake pan.
6. Pour half the batter into the cake pan, spread half of the apple pieces and half of the blackberries on top of the batter.
7. Add the remaining batter, covering most of the apple pieces and blackberries.
8. Spread the remaining half of the apple pieces and blackberries and any juices on top. Cover the cake pan tightly with aluminium foil.
9. Place cake pan onto trivet, add to the inner pot with 1 cup/250 ml of cold water.
10. Place lid on Instant Pot, set valve to seal, select manual high pressure (pressure cook custom high on Evo Plus) for 60 minutes.
11. When Instant Pot beeps, press cancel. Allow natural pressure release until the pin drops, open the lid.
12. Carefully lift the trivet with the cake from the Instant Pot. Take the cake off the trivet, remove the foil, allow 15 minutes before removing the cake from the pan.
13. Sprinkle with caster sugar.

INGREDIENTS

- 1 cup/240 ml milk
- 7 tbsp sugar
- 6 egg yolks
- 1 tsp vanilla extract
- 1 cup/240 ml heavy/double cream

PREPARATION STEPS

1. Fill inner pot to ¾ full with hot water. Select sous vide mode custom 85 °/c/185 °/f, set time for 1 hour and bring up to temperature.

2. In a bowl add 1 cup of milk, 7 tbsp sugar, 6 egg yolks and 1 tsp vanilla extract. Mix until sugar has dissolved.

3. Add 1 cup/240 ml heavy/double cream. Stir to combine.

4. Pour the mixture into 1 large or 2 small (for ease of handling) sous vide compatible zipper type bags.

5. Remove as much of the air as you can by lowering the bag(s) into a bowl of water, using the water to push the air out of the bag, being careful not to allow any water into the bag. Seal while immersed or use a vacuum sealer.

6. Once up to temperature, cook for 1 hour.

7. Strain into a jug and serve hot, or store refrigerated for up to 3 days.

Sous Vide Custard

A fool proof way to make custard.

SERVES 4

Sous Vide Crème Brûlée

Sous vide mode takes the stress out of making this dessert.

SERVES 2

INGREDIENTS

- 5 large egg yolks
- 3 ½ tbsp granulated sugar
- Pinch of salt
- 1 ¼ cup/300 ml whipping /heavy cream
- ½ vanilla bean
- 4 tsp demerara sugar

PREPARATION STEPS

1. Fill inner pot to maximum with hot water.
2. Select sous vide mode custom 82 °/c/179 °/f, bring up to temperature.
3. In the meantime, cut the vanilla bean in half lengthways and scrape out the seeds.
4. Whisk together 5 large egg yolks, 3 ½ tbsp granulated sugar and a pinch of salt.
5. Whisk in 1 ¼ cup/300 ml whipping/heavy cream and the vanilla seeds.
6. Strain custard through a fine mesh strainer into a jug.
7. Pour into a zipper type bag.
8. Remove as much of the air as you can by lowering the bag into a bowl of water, using the water to push the air out of the bag, being careful not to allow any water into the bag. Seal while immersed or use a vacuum sealer.
9. Once up to temperature, set timer for 30 minutes.
10. Lower the bag into the Instant Pot.
11. Close the lid making sure pressure valve is open. (remove silicone seal from lid if tainted with food odours).
12. When timer has finished, press cancel.
13. While custard is still hot, remove bag, cut off the corner and squeeze straight from the bag into your favourite ramekins.
14. Transfer ramekins to a wire rack, cover and let cool to room temperature, (about one hour). Refrigerate until chilled, (at least four hours).
15. Sprinkle 4 tbsp of demerara sugar evenly over each custard and wipe the rims of ramekins clean.
16. Use a kitchen blow torch, caramelise the sugar by sweeping the flame of the torch from the perimeter of the custard towards the middle, keeping the flame about 2 inches above the ramekin until sugar is bubbling and deep golden brown.
17. Let sit for 2 minutes to allow sugar crust to harden.
18. Serve immediately as sugar crust will soften after 20 minutes.

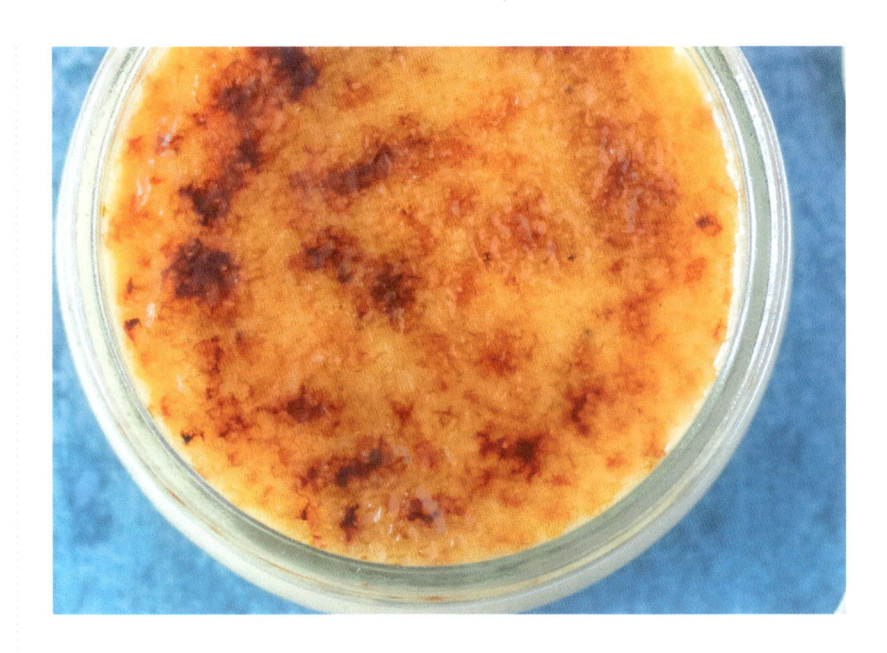

PREPARATION STEPS

1. Fill inner pot to ¾ full with hot water. Select sous vide mode custom 85 °/c/185 °/f, set time for 1 hour and bring up to temperature.

2. In a bowl add 1 cup/240 ml of milk, 7 tbsp sugar, 6 egg yolks and 1 tsp vanilla extract. Mix until sugar has dissolved.

3. Add 1 cup/240 ml heavy/double cream. Stir to combine.

4. Pour the mixture into 1 large or 2 small (for ease of handling) sous vide compatible zipper type bags.

5. Remove as much of the air as you can by lowering the bag into a bowl of water, using the water to push the air out of the bag, being careful not to allow any water into the bag. Seal while immersed or use a vacuum sealer.

6. Once up to temperature, cook for 1 hour.

7. After 1 hour, remove the bag(s) and submerge them in a 50/50 mix of ice and water for 1 hour.

8. Transfer to a refrigerator to chill for 8 hours or overnight.

9. Once the custard has cooled, strain it through a sieve into a jug then pour into an ice cream maker, churn according to the manufacturer's instructions.

10. Alternatively, to make the ice cream without an ice cream maker, pour the custard into a plastic container with a tight fitting lid.

11. Place in the freezer for 30 minutes.

12. After 30 minutes, remove from the freezer, use a fork or small whisk to mix the frozen custard from the outside to the middle.

13. Return to the freezer for a further 30 minutes, repeat the mixing process, breaking up any large pieces as you go.

14. Repeat these steps until the ice cream is evenly frozen. This will take around 3 to 4 hours.

15. Serve straight away or leave in the freezer to eat later.

Sous Vide Ice Cream

A fool proof way to make custard then turn it into ice cream.

SERVES 4

INGREDIENTS

- 1 cup/240 ml milk
- 7 tbsp sugar
- 6 egg yolks
- 1 tsp vanilla extract
- 1 cup/240 ml heavy/double cream

Chocolate Mousse

Naughty but nice.

SERVES 6

INGREDIENTS

- 7 oz/200g dark chocolate min 70% cocoa (cut into pieces)
- ½ cup/50g icing/powdered sugar
- ½ cup/120ml heavy/whipping cream (whipped)
- 4 large eggs (at room temperature for 2 hours then separated)
- ½ tsp cream of tartar

PREPARATION STEPS

1. Select sous vide mode custom 50 °/c/122 °/f, set minimum time and bring up to temperature.
2. Add 7 oz/200g dark chocolate min 70% cocoa (cut into pieces) and ½ cup/50g icing/powdered sugar to the pot.
3. Melt, stirring regularly for about 4 minutes.
4. Press cancel, remove bowl from the heat and transfer the chocolate mixture into a separate bowl.
5. Stir into the bowl ½ cup/120 ml heavy/whipping cream (whipped) and reserved 4 egg yolks.
6. In a separate clean bowl whisk the four egg whites until foamy (this is hard work and time consuming done manually, I recommend using an electric whisk if you have one).
7. Add ½ tsp cream of tartar and beat until soft peaks form.
8. Add whisked egg whites to reserved chocolate mixture and carefully fold using a spatula.
9. Pour into six individual desert bowls and refrigerate for at least three hours before serving.

2. Add 1 1/3 cup/200g soft dried figs, 2 tbsp light muscovado sugar and enough boiling water to just cover the fruit.
3. Bring to a boil, then cook for 15 minutes stirring occasionally until the figs are soft and the mixture is thick.
4. Transfer the mixture to a food processor or use a hand blender and blitz to a paste. Add 1 tsp ground cinnamon and 1 ball of stem ginger in syrup (drained), pulse for a few seconds to combine.
5. Spread the mixture onto a plate to cool.
6. Activate the yeast by heating 2 tbsp/30 ml of the milk to 46 °/c/115 °/f in the microwave. Transfer to a small bowl and stir in 2 tsp active dried yeast and ½ tsp of the granulated sugar. Let sit for five minutes.
7. Make the dough in a large bowl, whisk together 1 1/3 cup/160g all-purpose/plain flour, 1 ¼ tsp baking powder, remaining 2 ½ tsp of granulated sugar, and 1/3 tsp salt. Mix in 1 tbsp of the unsalted butter, ½ cup/125 ml whole milk and yeast mixture to form a rough dough.
8. Transfer the dough to a well-floured surface and knead until dough is soft and springy for about 3 minutes.
9. Re-flour the surface and roll the dough into a ¼ inch/0.6 cm thick rectangle measuring about 10 x 6 inches/25 x 15 cm. Turn the rectangle so that the long side is facing you. Brush with remaining 1 tbsp unsalted butter. Spread filling mixture across the dough.
10. Roll up the dough and slice into 6 equal rolls.
11. Transfer 1 roll to each of the 6 small glass heat resistant jars with screw tops (greased with oil or butter). Cover jars with clean kitchen towel and rest at room temperature for 30 minutes.
12. After 30 minutes, place the lids on the jars and seal until just tight, do not overtighten jars, air will still need to escape. Place into inner pot.
13. Fill inner pot with enough hot water to cover the jars.
14. Select sous vide mode custom 90 °/c/195 °/f, set time for 3 hours.
15. Place a heat resistant plate or lid over the jars to stop them from floating.
16. When the timer beeps, remove the jars from the pot and transfer to a cooling rack. Carefully remove the lids. Let the rolls cool for 5 minutes before running a knife around the side of the jars to remove.
17. Turn out or alternatively eat straight from the jar topped up with cream, custard, or ice cream.

Sous Vide Fig Swirls

Self-indulgence served hot straight from the jar.... topped up with cream.

SERVES 6

INGREDIENTS

- 6 x small glass heat resistant jars with screw tops (greased with oil or butter)

Filling

- 1 1/3 cup/200g soft dried figs
- 2 tbsp light muscovado sugar
- 1 tsp ground cinnamon
- 1 ball of stem ginger in syrup (drained)

Dough

- ½ cup/125 ml + 2 tbsp/30 ml milk
- 2 tsp active dried yeast
- 3 tsp granulated sugar
- 1 1/3 cup/160g all-purpose/plain flour
- 1 ¼ tsp baking powder
- 1/3 tsp salt
- 2 tbsp unsalted butter

PREPARATION STEPS

1. Press the sauté button on the Instant Pot on low heat, (custom level 2 for the Evo Plus).

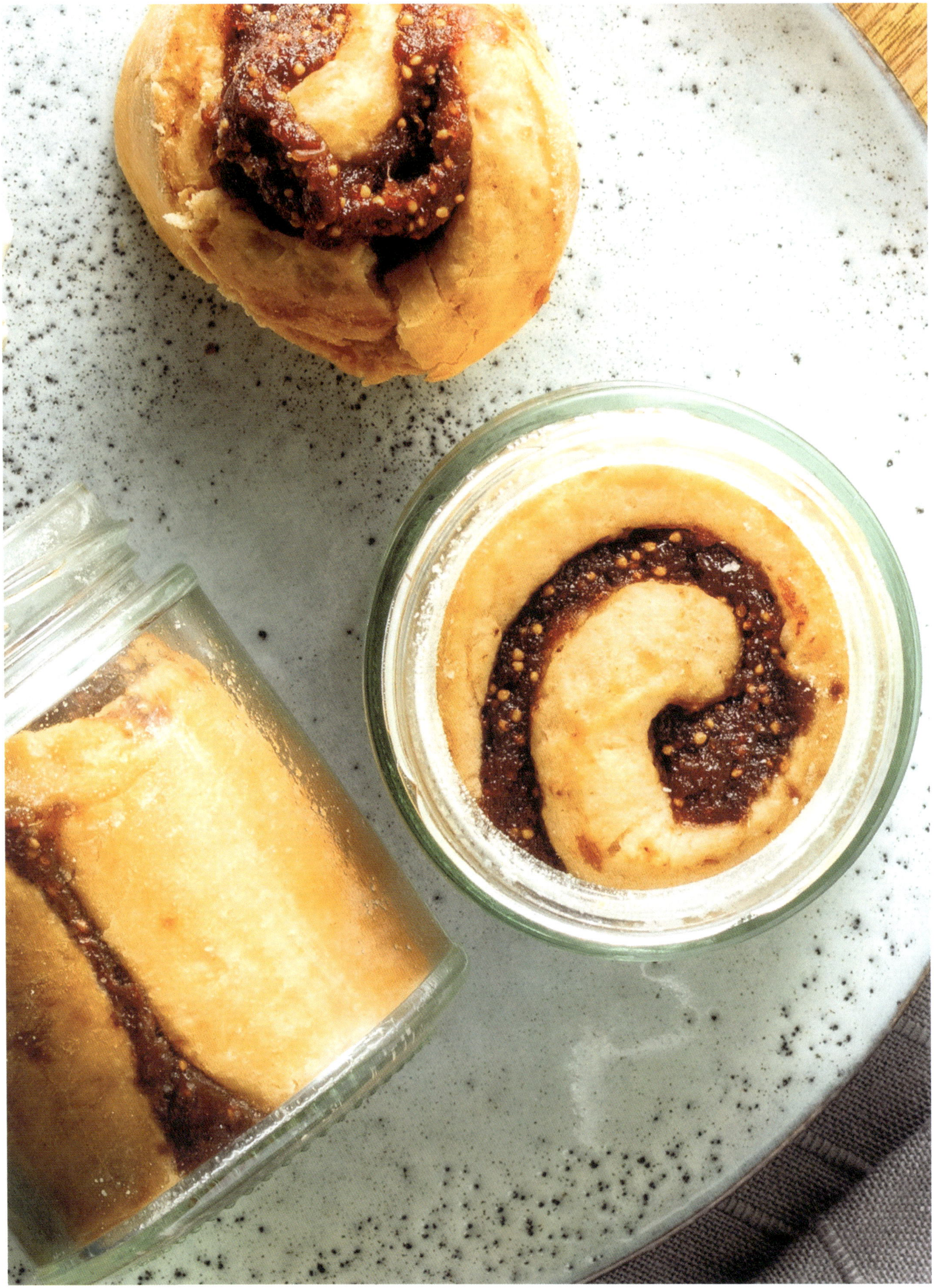

Sous Vide Tempered Chocolate

A reliable way to temper chocolate in sous vide mode.

INGREDIENTS

- Good quality (preferably couverture) dark or milk chocolate containing cocoa butter

PREPARATION STEPS

1. Select sous vide mode custom 48 °/c/120 °/f for dark chocolate 40 °/c/105 °/f for milk and white chocolate. Set 30 minutes and bring up to temperature.

2. Break the chocolate up into small chunks and add 3/4 to the inner pot. Let the chocolate gradually melt, stirring slowly and continuously.

3. When melted press cancel, remove the inner pot, and add the remaining chocolate a little at a time. Slowly stirring the chocolate each time until it melts, stopping when the temperature drops to 27 °/c/81 °/f. You can place the inner pot into some ice water to speed up the cooling process while you are stirring, but do not let any water get into the chocolate.

4. Place the inner pot back into the Instant Pot, select sous vide mode custom 31 °/c/88 °/f for dark chocolate, 30 °/c/85 °/f for milk and white chocolate.

5. Once up to temperature, spread a small spoonful of the chocolate on a piece of wax paper and place in the fridge for five minutes, if it looks dull or streaky or doesn't snap when you break it, re-temper the chocolate, starting at step 1. If it dries quickly with a gloss finish and no streaks, the chocolate is in temper.

6. Once melted chocolate has been tempered, it must be shaped/set in mould before it cools and sets. If it cools to about 29 °/c/84 °/f and is still fairly liquid, it can be reheated to a liquid consistency. If it has completely cooled and solidified, it should be re-tempered starting at step 1.

7. The Instant Pot will keep the temperature of the chocolate much more consistent than using a bain-marie, giving you more time to work with the chocolate.

Acknowledgments

I would like to thank my partner Kathy for putting up with all the craziness in the kitchen, my absences when out shopping and writing, for always being supportive, and encouraging me when I started to run out of steam (Instant Pot joke).

To James, it's been nice to have an excuse to spend so much time with you. Your knowledge has been such a great asset to this book.

Thank you to my other children, Anna-Louise, Victoria, and Adam. Whose help was always at hand.

Lastly, thanks to my sister Sheila, for always holding things together.

G.S.

Printed in Great Britain
by Amazon